# THE
# ROYAL OPERA HOUSE
## COVENT GARDEN

# THE
# ROYAL
# OPERA
# HOUSE
## COVENT GARDEN

Photographs by
## CLIVE BOURSNELL
Picture~edited by Mia Stewart~Wilson

Text by
## COLIN THUBRON

Design by Craig Dodd
# HAMISH HAMILTON
London

To my parents
Ray and Vera Boursnell

The original hardback publication of this book was generously sponsored by

Commercial Union Assurance

First published in Great Britain 1982 by
Hamish Hamilton Limited
Garden House 57–59 Long Acre London WC2E 9JZ
First published in this edition 1984

British Library Cataloguing in Publication Data
Boursnell, Clive
The Royal Opera House.
1. Royal Opera House History
I. Title    II. Thubron, Colin
782.1'0942132    PN2596.L7/R
ISBN 0–241–10891–8
ISBN 0–241–11188–9 Pbk

Printed in Great Britain by Jolly & Barber Ltd, Rugby

# CONTENTS

Foreword by
HRH The Prince of Wales 7

Photographer's Introduction 8

THE HOUSE 12

BEGINNINGS 54

IN THE STUDIO 100

ON STAGE 141

PERFORMANCE 190

Index 255

Acknowledgements 256

# FOREWORD BY
## HRH THE PRINCE OF WALES

It is extraordinary how much we take for granted in the world about us. Until I became Patron of The Royal Opera and involved in the Development Appeal I had absolutely no idea of what really went on at Covent Garden. If you go to the opera or to the ballet you are swept up into the exciting atmosphere of the opera house, engendered by the red and gold surroundings and the feeling of being somewhere rather special. Thoughts of what might be going on backstage or of how such a dazzling and professional performance is organized are far from your mind. But, as this book describes, the contrast between the front and back of the house is very surprising indeed.

A tour around the backstage areas reveals a hive of seemingly chaotic activity which even stretches into the streets outside, and beyond, into neighbouring buildings with teams of people shifting and storing scenery in pantechnicons because there is no room in the actual opera house. The conditions in which everyone works are indeed archaic and somewhat squalid, but as so often paradoxically happens in these circumstances they produce an extraordinary spirit of improvisation and a corresponding sense of British humour, which blossoms when people are faced with what others might consider to be insurmountable problems. Now that the redevelopment of the area behind the opera house stage is under way – and indeed phase 1 is virtually complete – those who work in the house can look forward to something far more practical and efficient. Apart from anything else there will now be suitable practice rooms for the singers and, we hope, rat-free washing rooms for the chorus.

After 250 years The Royal Opera House is one of this country's grand old institutions. So many famous names have trodden its boards; so much talent and artistic perfection has been seen and heard; so much pleasure and, indeed, inspiration, has been given to countless numbers of people of all ages whose successors will continue to revel in the glorious sounds of the human voice and in the expressive movements of the dance. What I say next may be a rather worn-out old cliché, but I am still going to repeat it! Without the benefit of such artistic expression – of a very high standard – our inner selves would become arid and meaningless. We therefore have to have the will and the means to ensure not just the survival of this famous institution, but also its continued growth and development. Those of us who have a deep affection for The Opera House, and all it means, are determined to see that this happens.

# PHOTOGRAPHER'S
# INTRODUCTION

Late in 1978, with the help of Sergeant Martin, I often stood at the back of the stalls circle of the House. There, my love of opera and ballet deepened. I began to realise that I wanted to know much more about life and work in the House – what gets that curtain up at 7.30 every night? How does it all happen? I felt that, through my photography, I might be able to tell some of the story.

I had just begun working with Leica cameras, which are unobtrusive and comfortable to hold. As the idea of a behind-the-scenes photographic book crystallised, I bullied a friend to let me have his M4 Leica, with an F1 50mm lens. For my purposes this was the perfect combination – a near-silent camera which would not disturb artists and craftsmen at work in the House, together with a fast lens, so that I did not have to push the film and could keep a high quality of tones and detail in the photographs, in spite of working in difficult and very low light-level conditions.

Sir John Tooley unleashed me on the House in June 1979. It took the first nine months not only for me to get to know them all, but more importantly, for them to get to know and ignore me, although I know I was often in the way.

On no single occasion did I set up or tolerate any posed play to my camera. What I missed, I missed; and the blurred fleeting moment was caught – blurred! Through my photographs, I at first tried to describe fully the many different shows on which the House was working, each at a different stage but all at the same time. My picture editor, Mia Stewart-Wilson, and I then found that each production was simply a part of the grand pattern – without beginning or end – of a great theatre at work. So we have included some – but not all – of the productions I have worked on, illustrating the different aspects of this single story. I shot an immense amount of film and editing this down to a book of 256 pages took four painful and exciting months. The final selection and the vision of the daily workings of the House which it represents are our own.

I have photographed nearly everyone at some time or another, and I pray that those people not in the book will not feel hurt or left out for being sacrificed for what I hope is a good story and not just a *Who's Who*. Colin Thubron and I would like to thank all of you by name, for without your goodwill it would not have been possible to get very far, let alone to take the book to completion. As there are nearly 1,100 of you working at the House, plus visiting artists, it is impossible to name all of you. However, many of you were absolutely indispensable in the help you afforded us. Where *does* one start?

Thank you, Sir John Tooley for the courage to let me loose on the House. For help and advice far in excess of what we could have expected: Sir Frederick Ashton, John Copley, Sir Colin Davis, Kensington Davison, David Edwards, Paul Findlay, Ron Freeman, Götz Friedrich, Keith Gray, Robin Hambro, Trevor Jones, Iris Law, Tom Macarthur, Bill McGee, Kenneth MacMillan, Monica Mason, Peter Morrell, Elijah Moshinsky,

William Ould, Jeffrey Phillips, Patrick Pursey, Ted Pursey, Helga Schmidt, Edward Slaymaker, Michael Somes, Reg Suter, Brian Swan, Michael Thomson, John Walker, Katharine Wilkinson. And thanks to The Board of the Royal Opera House, Governors of The Royal Ballet and Trustees of the Royal Opera House Trust. To Stella Chitty, when she had made up her mind that she approved of the project – thank you, Stella. Thank you for the help I received daily from every member of The Royal Ballet and The Royal Opera Companies and their visiting artists, from the orchestra and their conductors and from all members of the House staff. The names of the many others to whom we are especially grateful are listed at the end of the book.

Special thanks to Sir Francis Sandilands of the Commercial Union Assurance for financial assistance to my publishers, Hamish Hamilton. To Craig Dodd for his sympathy to my work. To Richard Davies, for putting up with me in our dark room and for endless supportive lunches.

To Mia Stewart-Wilson, who has been of the greatest support to the book for two years with her ability to grasp my objectives, her clear-sighted editing and power to cut through my dilemmas and occasional depression over the project. Mia, I shall always be deeply indebted to you.

I cannot begin to describe the effect that the last three years of music-drama and dance have had upon me. No matter what I go on to do, or where I go to do it, this time will always stay with me and be very much part of me. Thank you, The Royal Opera House.

Clive Boursnell
June 1982

# THE HOUSE

The very name – 'the Royal Opera House, Covent Garden' – emits an inscrutable scent of vegetables and majesty. The theatre rises from dilapidated streets with the naturalness of something ageless and unplanned. It is huge, serene, reticently handsome – a great white quinquireme of a building, cruising among irregular waves of lanes. Far into the eighteenth century this neighbourhood was the haunt of coffee-house literati and the theatrical demi-monde, and it still exudes a faintly raffish independence. Nothing suggests that here was once the garden of a convent in Westminster, which passed to the Bedford family after the dissolution of the monasteries.

As you enter the foyer, the ghosts come thronging about you. Your feet fall silent on a lilac-coloured carpet which pervades the whole house. Busts of Patti and Melba gaze across from the inner doors. Such phantoms linger incalculably in the air – Patti waltzing through the ball scene of *La traviata* with 3,700 diamonds glistening on her white dress (and two detectives in the chorus); Chaliapin fumbling his cues and ordering the conductor to hurry up in the middle of *Faust*; the Tosca of Callas and the Scarpia of Gobbi, incarnate fire and stone; Fonteyn dancing Aurora before George VI as the house reopened after the Second World War at the dawn of the new peace.

This past has leaked into the theatre's foundations, and has invested it with the character and challenge of a living organism. Its inner workings are so complex that they are all but unknown to outsiders. The question nags: what does it do? Its offspring of operas and ballets is ceaselessly criticised or loved, but their long birth-pangs go almost unrecorded.

Even its history lends it a glamorous strangeness. Ever since 1732, when the actor-manager John Rich opened his newly-built Theatre Royal here, the site has been filled with drama on and off the stage. Handel touched it with a brief operatic glory in the 1730s, and after a fire in 1808 had burnt it to the ground, the Prince Regent himself laid the second theatre's foundation stone – a hoary block which still slumbers in a corner of the basement wash-rooms. This neo-classical titan of a theatre – it was rumoured to be the largest in Europe – was converted into a true opera house in 1847, and after nine seasons of mingled financial disaster and musical triumph was swept away by fire after a disorderly fancy dress ball.

From these ashes, in a mere seven months, arose the present house. Designed by Edward Barry, son of the architect of the Houses of Parliament, it incorporated little of the past but some friezes by the sculptor Flaxman reset in the portico. From the moment of its foundation it played lavish host to the operatic singers and composers of the world. The reigns of Patti and Melba, the *Ring* cycles of Mahler and Richter, the debuts of the de Reszkes and Caruso, the seasons of Beecham and Bruno Walter – year after year the great theatre overflowed with music, spectacle and scandal, spilling into moments of near-eclipse – in the First World War it became a furniture warehouse, in the Second a palais de danse.

Such history is part of the house's mystique, its public aura. Its private face is less accessible. But the question persists: what does it do?

The front of the house offers no clue to such enigmas. It is steeped in the gracious safety of its past. To the left of the foyer the grand staircase mounts beneath allegorical paintings which throw up a mist of trees and paradise-birds. At its head the audience from the grand tier and balcony congregates in the Crush Bar at evening. A single chandelier hovers above – a cataract of diamond lights – and along the west wall, in twenty-foot-high paintings, classical divinities loll among cupids, who steal their goblets or suck impertinently at their breasts. Only when the people have gone are these reception rooms seen to be agreeably down-at-heel, the carpet patched, the wallpaper scuffed here and there. They are redolent of age, experience, compromise.

But it is the auditorium which is the glory of the place. If it cannot match the brilliance of the Bolshoi or La Scala's imperial spaciousness or the jewel-like radiance of the Fenice, it breathes out a restrained beauty all its own. Its horseshoe tiers rise in a soft conflagration of crimson, cream and gold. Above them the amphitheatre's six hundred seats spread far back into dimness, while at the building's summit a shallow blue dome floats in a disc of lights. Above the stage, on a gold tympanum, Orpheus and Ossian play the lyre to bucolic listeners in white bas-relief, while down the proscenium beneath, forty feet high and forty-five feet wide, the three-ton curtains rest in a shining fall of claret-red velvet embroidered with the royal monogram.

As early as 1892, the auditorium lights were converted from gas to electricity. Now, all along the serpentine tier-fronts more than a hundred red-shaded candelabra shine, while above each one lounges a female genie with a faintly insolent smile. These demi-mermaids (their bodies taper into scaley herbage) mature and degenerate as they descend from the amphitheatre. In the uppermost semicircle they masquerade as Christian cupids with regulation wings and trumpets, but below the balcony and the grand tier they slide into a heathen pubescence; their shoulders sprout enigmatic butterfly wings and they lean back on their tiers with pagan sorcery, their arms bangled, their breasts bare and their waists merging into inscrutable vegetable matter.

The audience seated in this idolatrous glamour has changed more than its surroundings. Gone are the days when Berlioz was refused entry to his seat because the colour of his evening coat and trousers did not match, or when the auditorium lights were left full on so that the 'nobility and gentry' could comment on each other's clothes and consorts. (As late as the 1950s programmes carried a request that ladies remove their hats.) The ranks of private boxes which once circled the house have been whittled to twenty-four, raising the total seat capacity to 2,158, while the amphitheatre and the once-spartan gallery were merged comfortably in 1964 after the columns beneath them were found to have been weakened by the drumming (it is thought) of enthusiastic feet.

Signs of luxury, in any case, were never flagrant. The royal box, centrepiece of Continental houses, occupies a discreet place to one side. It is served by a small suite on two storeys, entered from a private door in neighbouring Floral Street. On the ground floor, in the King's Smoking Room, whose low, coffered ceilings and cramped proportions may have been modelled on those of a saloon in the royal yacht, a narrow stairway (now blocked) ascends to the stage, so that the more artistic or libidinous royalty could ask ballerinas and singers to visit them in private. A little alcove sofa, sheltered under a baldachino, is resonant with vanished intimacies.

The box itself (reserved first for Royalty, then for the opera house directors) is reached by another stair, where Hockney's portrait of Sir David Webster, General Administrator of the house for twenty-five years, sets him staring into nothing beside a vase of painted tulips, defying explication. Beyond, a cool casket of an anteroom, white and pale blue, is ringed by white chairs from Windsor Castle and attended by an elegant mahogany lavatory, while the box itself is still furnished with armchairs for Queen Victoria and Prince Albert and hung with a mirror on one side so that ladies-in-waiting could watch performances reflected. Only the adjoining Bedford box, its suite decorated in green and gold, can match this hushed precinct. The Bedfords' easy-going motto – 'Che Sara Sara' – remains inscribed above the marble mantelpiece, although the box has passed from their ownership.

Such serene enclaves of privilege reflect in microcosm all the public part of the house. An aura of chaste intimacy pervades it. It encircles the stage with an unchanging beauty which subtly suggests that everything – dance, singing, orchestra, scenery – must unroll with the same harmonious logic as its own tiers and stairs.

But step backstage, and the illusion is gone. The gilded spaces of the auditorium disintegrate into a skein of seedy rooms and beetling corridors. Worn stone stairways lumber down between walls chipped and stained; lifts clank in their steel cages; and a hundred constricted passageways wriggle and bifurcate and converge again like worms through an over-ripe cheese. As you wander through these disfigured rooms – compressed to niches or attenuated to threads – you have the sensation of circling some unreachable void. For at the core of the building lies the great concavity of stage and auditorium, which presses everything else into peripheral slivers and crannies. Directors and managers occupy mere footholds and interstices in this huge creature's body – wizened offices where the lilac carpet erupts again, thin and discoloured. In summer the basement corridors are steamy with heat like the bowels of an ocean liner; pipes and cables squirm overhead and the curve of some passageways, as they follow the arc of the auditorium above them, might be tracing the trajectory of a monstrous prow.

Working conditions here are worse than in any other great opera house in the world. Only the new extension, completed in the spring of 1982, releases the labyrinth into the sudden airiness of opera and ballet studios, a chorus rehearsal room, new wardrobe and dressing areas. The old dressing facilities have been a scandal for years. The principal ballet dancers still occupy two ranges of cramped rooms, furnished with little but basins and communal showers. In these cubicles some of the world's finest dancers eke out the tensions of intervals and debuts, while beneath them, in mazey chambers of their own, the *corps de ballet* stares at itself in unflattering lengths of mirror, sitting cheek by jowl on plastic-topped chairs.

Nowhere is there any space. Walking down remote passages, you snake among sheaves of operatic spears and crates of champagne, or blunder into hampers packed with the puritanical casques and breastplates of *Luisa Miller* or tutus for *Swan Lake*. Only as you climb higher in the building – five, six, seven storeys up – does the clutter thin away. Momentarily the space-hung fly galleries, lined with ropes and cables, give a glimpse of the stage far below, then the stairs ascend again to a fetid loft where heating and ventil-

*Opposite: retouching the profile of Queen Victoria above the proscenium arch and repairing the auditorium carpet, whose design is said to have been suggested by Sir Thomas Beecham*

ation units throb and whine and send fat, visceral-looking air tubes winding beneath the house's skylit roof.

This backstage jumble inflicts its intimacy on all concerned, and arouses affection as well as disgust. It reminds Placido Domingo of his youth, and makes him feel at home; and Kiri te Kanawa, who is unnerved by grand dressing-rooms, finds that its shambling humanity preserves her confidence. But others are disorientated at stepping from such squalor into the luxurious fantasy of most grand opera on stage. 'It creates a kind of culture shock,' says Grace Bumbry. 'I like to get into the feeling of what I'm about to do, and here I can't.' Whereas Stuart Burrows is afflicted simply by the poor ventilation, which grinds people's tempers thin and sends the makeup streaming down his face.

The opera house, in any case, affords its artists only spurious rest. All its rooms, even the lavatories, are connected by loudspeaker to the control panel in the stage wings. The stage is the nerve-centre and altar of the house. There is no escaping it. In the mezzanine behind the orchestra pit, where the cases for the double-basses loom like ranks of pharaonic coffins, the colossal frame on which its boards are set rises from concrete basements in a brooding forest of black steel. From here, by many cables and wheels, the whole central platform can be electrically raised or lowered some eight feet in five giant sections.

These near-soundless lifts, constructed more than seventy years ago, grow up from the very deeps of the house. Above them the stage resounds to every footfall. Beneath them, in a huge, twilit gallery of the cellars, the scenic cloths for hundreds of operas and ballets rest in dust-glazed heaps, sixty feet long or more. Even some pieces from the 1899 production of *La Bohème*, which was only superseded in 1974, linger on in a back dock of the house, haunted by Melba and Caruso.

As for the stage itself, it fatally echoes this overcrowdedness. When the house was planned in 1858, it was designed for short opera seasons, often staged by visiting impresarios. Had it been built even a few years later, it might have enjoyed the wing-breadth of the Paris Opéra. As it is, its fifty-foot-square acting area is flanked by wings only twenty feet wide, where the scenic flats are heaped one against the next in the interstices between electrical and carpentry docks. Although the working stage runs over eighty feet deep, its back recesses are overhung by an enormous paint studio which drops its finished canvases to racks below, and the begrimed walls are so stacked with current scenery that they show only patches of whitewashed brick high up, pocked with enigmatic niches and blind windows. Far above the stage a liana jungle of cloths, bars and light battens is still controlled from the fly galleries by an antiquated system of counterweights, and is girdled by a rolling cyclorama installed in 1933 – the same great hemicycle that floods the skies of *Otello* with storm-clouds or circles *Madama Butterfly* in a night awash with stars.

Today the Metropolitan in New York and the great German and Austrian houses are equipped with side and rear stages on which complete sets can be pre-built. Almost at the push of a button, an auxiliary stage can be wheeled by thin tracks onto the central acting area, which is fractionally lowered. Compared to this, the Royal Opera House was designed merely to receive the rolled backcloths and one-dimensional scenery of early Victorian years. Most of its machinery was installed in 1901, when the grid roof was raised to seventy-three feet above the newly flattened boards.

Everywhere it is claustrophobically cramped. Behind the same gold proscenium arch which the audience sees, five banks of lamps and three tiers of iron gangways beetle and leer from one end to the other, and merge along the jambs with whole batteries of other lamps, dangling in drifts and clusters among half-lit ladders and electrical perches. The surface of the stage itself, although it incorporates five huge elevators and five trap doors, has been adapted for ballet. Just beneath its fifteen-millimetre skin of birch plywood, and above the oak beams and massive steel framework on which the whole floor rests, spreads a thin, springy cushion of rubber. So different are the needs of opera and ballet that this is too soft easily to receive the screwed-in tracks on which some heavy operatic scenery runs, and must be replaced piecemeal for the safety of dancers as ponderous scene changes wear away its veneer or gouge its panels.

For the theatre now supports two resident companies – The Royal Opera and The Royal Ballet, which was incorporated into the house in 1946 – and probably it achieves more with worse facilities than any comparable institution in the world. On any one morning six or seven different halls or studios are reverberating to operatic *fioriture*, orchestral crescendoes or pirouettes and *tours en l'air*. The female section of the chorus, perhaps, ensconced in its new rehearsal room, is managing *Eugene Onegin* in Russian, while the male is singing *Billy Budd* in another hall nearby. In the main opera studio the principals for *Tristan und Isolde* are striding about makeshift sets; soloists for *The Rake's Progress* practise in a room off Floral Street opposite; and on the stage itself, crowded with scene-shifters, the forest cottage of *Giselle* is replacing the suicide scene for *Werther*.

In the ballet studios, meanwhile, either here or at the Royal Ballet headquarters in Barons Court, or both, the company performs its morning class. 'Stretch the arabesque . . . plié . . . stretch up, *right* up . . . five and six and back to *attitude*. . . .' The voice is Gerd Larsen's, teaching the bitter-sweet ritual of being graceful. She claps her hands. The girls speed up. 'Stretch your legs . . . and jeté. . . .' At the same time the orchestra is rehearsing beneath the ormolued lights and chandeliers of the Crush Bar. Crammed into this gold and crimson glory, and watched by a bust of Sir Thomas Beecham whose raised baton seems about to usurp control, it appears to have assembled for some elaborate soirée, at which the guests are unaccountably absent.

All these activities involve a bewildering diversity of people – a payroll of over 1,000, split between three unions (Equity, the Musicians' Union and NATTKE), grumblingly British, sensitive and sometimes divided, but affectionate and loyal to itself. Its heterogeneous employees – stage hands, electricians, repetiteurs, violinists, baritones, coryphées, costumiers, cleaners – converge on a charmless canteen in the theatre's basement. On dress rehearsal days, or in the evenings, the place takes on a lunatic air. A sable- and jewel-trimmed Byzantine court or a flock of cygnets in leotards can be seen regaling itself with chips or yoghourt, operatic nuns swill beer in the adjoining green room, and Renaissance courtiers hot-foot from *Lucrezia Borgia* break into Welsh dialect or sing falsetto limericks at the bar.

The disciplines rarely mix. The orchestra, skilled through application and intellect, sits divorced from the raucous good humour of the singers, blessed by a pure gift, who fill the air with their broad and beautiful regional accents. And neither mingles with the dancers, possessors of fierce wills and accurate bodies, who are quiet and contained, as if their art owned them.

These informal minglings and isolations are reflected in the outside offices too. The scenery-building, the making of the stage properties and much of the cloth-painting are executed in distant workshops, and storehouses for scenery and costumes are scattered all over London and even in Kent. In a jumbled range of buildings along Floral Street, colloquially called '45' and '51', the financial and overall administration, costume work-rooms, repetiteurs' studios, press and box offices, model and design rooms, dye vats, headquarters for advertising and marketing, offices of the Friends of Covent Garden (whose membership by 1982 had reached 15,000), subsidiary ballet offices and music libraries (where scores are altered or transposed for whole casts and orchestras) – all these and myriad others are crowded and interlaced together. The corridors are turned into defiles and culs-de-sac by wicker baskets packed with skirts for *La sonnambula* or houp-pelandes for *The Sleeping Beauty*, and near the carpenters' and electricians' workshops a storage basement is stuffed with leering plaster statues, candelabra, oscillating skeletons, fake foliage, dolls, panpipes, in a farrago of styles and centuries which looks as if it could never be used again. In the house archives the letters come down the years from Mario, Grisi and Patti (with cartoons by Caruso) to the confidential files of Sir David Webster

*The orchestra rehearsing in the Crush Bar, with Ashley Lawrence*

A chorus rehearsal, above, and The Royal Ballet at the barre, left, in the Crush Bar before the opening of the extension studios in 1982

(not yet available); and its gamut of twentieth-century stage designs includes eleven hundred costume sketches by Attilio Comelli (discovered on top of a disused cupboard), drawings by Visconti and Zeffirelli, and Salvador Dali's paintings for his scandalous 1949 *Salome* produced by Peter Brook.

This apparent chaos – all the obsolescence of premises and paucity of means – demands, of course, a compensating human efficiency. Activity grows more, not less. The house's responsibilities embrace not only the two main companies but the wardrobe, stage furnishings and financial administration of the 50-strong Sadler's Wells Royal Ballet, which occupies its own theatre in Rosebery Avenue and undertakes a prodigious touring schedule.

The General Director of this polymorphic musical empire, Sir John Tooley, falls heir to a stability of stewardship almost unknown to Continental opera houses. His only predecessor since the war, Sir David Webster, ruled for twenty-five years with the distant and avuncular autocracy of one of the shrewder Mogul emperors. John Tooley, his assistant for fifteen years, is industrious and accessible. He sits at a modest desk in one corner of a modest boardroom. Directors for administration and finance stem the torrent of incoming bureaucracy to a bearable stream, and his deputy, Paul Findlay, supervises public affairs and touring. Sir John Tooley involves himself intensely in the workings of the house, inspects every scenic model, inhabits the stage and auditorium during rehearsals (as a young man he longed to be a singer), travels constantly to the Continent and the States. His inclination is to be calm, placatory, steering his policies among the reefs of trade unions and international opera houses, Arts Council and business trustees. The day of the autocrat is gone.

He is supported by a formidable Board of thirteen directors under the chairmanship of banker Sir Claus Moser and the secretaryship of Sir Robert Armstrong, Secretary to the Cabinet. These are not only watchdogs over the public's money but translate the opera house plans into financial terms and lobby the Arts Council. With Sir John Tooley they formulate new policy and take decisions on its wider issues – touring, allocation of funds, seat prices, the number of new productions per season; and they appoint the senior personnel, including the post of General Director itself. Every two months they split into opera, ballet and finance sub-committees, but their touch on production or musical matters is discreet.

In the mid-1960s, Sir David Webster's musical director, Sir Georg Solti, declared that he would make Covent Garden the finest opera house in the world, and today it stands with the Metropolitan, La Scala, the Viennese Staatsoper, the Paris Opéra and the Bolshoi in an echelon of unequalled accomplishment. The music directorship in 1971 passed into the gentle and democratic hands of Sir Colin Davis, already distinguished over a wide repertoire, especially for his Berlioz and Mozart interpretations. Together with Sir John Tooley, he has tried to preserve the excitement of the Solti era, but has altered its tone of voice. There is a new emphasis on youth. Week-long promenade seasons turn the usually staid orchestra stalls into a 700-strong bivouac of balletomanes and opera-lovers, and the Ballet's Big Top tent (dreamed up by Sir John Tooley during a chance conversation with Sir Michael Tippett) carries dance informally to towns with no large theatre. Television and radio transmissions falteringly grow (the televised *Die Fledermaus* reached many million viewers in a single transmission) and are now linked with a video cassette and record venture by which the BBC films performances and an independent company markets the results.

The annual press conference, at which the management announces its plans, with (left to right) Sir John Tooley, Sir Claus Moser and financial director Adrian Doran; the postal booking office; the opera press office; press photographers at a ballet dress rehearsal

Opposite top: meeting of the board of directors under chairman Sir Claus Moser, seated fifth from left with Sir John Tooley

Opposite bottom: governors of The Royal Ballet with their president, HRH Princess Margaret (third from right) beside Dame Ninette de Valois and Dame Alicia Markova

Yet finances are pitifully strained. Unsponsored touring is cruelly expensive, and it is a myth that the Royal Ballet tours in America make money. A large but unpredictable grant from the Arts Council (currently 53 per cent of the total revenue) contrasts sadly with comparable houses abroad. Many productions are made possible only by gifts from business sponsors, either individually or through a corporate Trust. The remaining 43 per cent comes from the box office.

Yet such stringent finances engendered the economical and lovely productions of *Peter Grimes* and *Lohengrin*. The yearly number of performances in the house exceeded three hundred in the 1979–80 season for the first time. And productions of modern opera are being intensified, despite the expense in rehearsal time and the box office risk. ('It costs so much to fail,' says Colin Davis, 'but it's possible, however remotely, that one of these operas will become part of the standard repertory, like *Peter Grimes* or *King Priam*.') John Tooley ideally envisages one commissioned work in each season, and has tried to save expense by links with foreign houses. The next ten years are replete with these bold and fragile ambitions: a Berio opera and Stockhausen's *Donnerstag* ; a work by Messiaen with the Paris Opéra; Edward Cowie's *Ned Kelly* (with designs by Sir Sidney Nolan); and operas by the Finnish composer Aulis Sallinen (with BBC Radio and the Savonlinna Festival), by Thea Musgrave and the Hungarian Gyorgy Ligeti. With all these there are hopes of building up the Slav, French and Wagner repertoire, of completing Donizetti's historical trilogy and of launching a Rossini festival.

As for The Royal Ballet, it cannot plan as The Royal Opera does. Its structure, in any case, is profoundly different. The Ballet is a close-knit, almost caste-like company; the Opera a sprawling international commitment. The Opera grazes on a huge field of resurrectable classics; the Ballet enjoys a mere handful, and must create its own. Those who love the one art do not always love the other.

But the Ballet has proved uniquely creative. Born of the vision and energy of Dame Ninette de Valois more than fifty years ago, grown up in the discipline of the Russian classics and in the limpid beauty of its native choreography, it commands a breadth of repertoire unequalled in the world. It was the dance invention of Sir Frederick Ashton, even in the 1930s, which expressed the company most perfectly, eliciting from it that 'English style' – lyrical, restrained, aristocratic – which has marked it ever since.

It is a company of strong pride but little vanity. Many of its dancers have known each other since early youth, and respect is earned hard. Its premises at Barons Court, sandwiched between the thunder of lorry traffic in front and the moan of underground trains behind, are muddled in with its own upper school, whose students, in their regulation black leotards and pink tights, rub shoulders with the company dancers and stare at their rehearsals through the glass-panelled doors. The days of automatic reverence have gone. Gone too is the six-day week of obligatory barre exercises (now reduced to four) and no gossiping in the passages.

But technical standards have risen savagely, and in these monastic studios, mirror-lined, inward-looking, the feeling remains of a relentless ritual of self-criticism, something private and absolute. The senior teachers – Michael Somes, Jill Gregory, Gerd Larsen – are priest-like perfectionists. They guard the classical heritage by which all technique is measured. When dancers stare in the mirror, it is not to admire but to correct; and it is perhaps their eternal pupilship and shared strain which lend them almost a family resemblance, a look of suspended youth.

The adaptability engendered by this classical training is the safeguard of the future. As the world of Ashton – its delicate romanticism, its sureness of values – slides irretrievably away, his successor as resident choreographer, Kenneth MacMillan, makes different physical and psychological demands; and slowly, subtly, the company style changes. This rupture is not a chance crisis but a sensitive reflection of the times. The muse of Ashton was Margot Fonteyn – reticent, lovely of line, the 'English style' incarnate; the chosen vessel of MacMillan was the rebelliously complex Lynn Seymour. Between the two – in dance and in life – a whole world passed away.

To sustain the diversity of the company yet preserve its wholeness; to cross-fertilise the classical, the neo-classical and the modern, mingling the loosely-called 'MacMillan dancer' and the 'Ashton dancer' – these are the preoccupations of the Royal Ballet's director, Norman Morrice. Like Colin Davis, he is less attuned to desk work than to the feeding of young talent in the studio (both men speak with delight of the artists they have nurtured) and Morrice has restricted the star system and concentrated instead on growth within the company. Running the risk of tension and jealousy, especially in the *corps de ballet*, he is giving star roles to dancers as they become ready, however young. This is a tribute to a hugely talented generation born around 1960 – Fiona Chadwick, Bryony Brind, Pippa Wylde and several boys. 'It's cruel to make them wait,' he says. 'They are oozing with talent. If you deny it, you can go beyond the point where it will flower.'

To such dancers the 1960s heyday of Fonteyn and Nureyev is not even a memory; and of that golden shoal of ballerinas which swam out from their shadow – Antoinette Sibley, Lynn Seymour, Merle Park, Monica Mason, Deanne Bergsma – only Park and Mason

*The Royal Ballet School: students watch the company*

are left. The company, once so rich in girls, is now blessed instead with ten or eleven male dancers whose styles range from that of Anthony Dowell, the prince of *danseurs nobles*, to the robust authority of David Wall, Wayne Eagling's half nonchalant bravura, and the daemonic onslaught of Stephen Jefferies, perhaps the finest actor-dancer of them all.

It is among the girls that the spectrum grows thin. Merle Park, so mellifluous of technique, is possibly top ballerina now; and Monica Mason, supremely musical and strong, invests her finest roles with a nobility all her own. But beyond these two it remains for Lesley Collier – vibrant, impregnably sound – and for Jennifer Penney to hold the ring; because thereafter, for a full fifteen years, it is chiefly Marguerite Porter who lends distinction to a landscape empty of world-class talent.

But the future is not as tentative as it seems. It brims with young promise. And the past holds up a standard which looms behind the uncertain present and comes down to dancers in illusive ways. Dancing is imitative; its teachers and performers have learnt by watching. Established roles are not inherited pure, but exist in a nimbus of memories and expectations, which may assume a tyrannical life of their own. In such a close-knit company as the Royal, the great performances are never definitively lost, but continue in an ever-failing yet pervasive inheritance. Like the sound of voices in another room, they cannot be quite discounted.

So Fonteyn dances again in every Aurora.

*Opposite: The Royal Ballet School*

Morning class with Monica Mason, left, Wayne Eagling and Karen Paisey, below, and members of the company, opposite

Overleaf: rehearsing *Swan Lake*: David Wall and Marguerite Porter

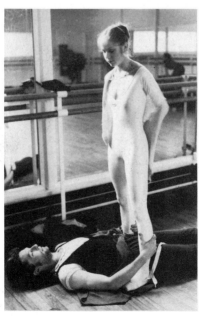

Gerd Larsen supervises morning class, with Jonathan
Frank at the piano

**Manon,** Act III. Christopher Newton as the Ratcatcher,
David Wall as Des Grieux

**Werther.** José Carreras with his agent during an interval

**Lulu.** Opposite: producer Götz Friedrich directing an early rehearsal

**Lulu**. Opposite above: Götz Friedrich at rehearsal, with designer Timothy O'Brien (left) and assistant producer Michael Rennison (right). Opposite below: Colin Davis in studio rehearsal with Glenys Linos, right (Countess Geschwitz) and Karan Armstrong (Lulu)

Above: Jeffrey Phillips, production manager (right), demonstrates scenery movement to the stage charge hands. Left: designer Timothy O'Brien, in the model room, explains scene changes to *Lulu*'s lighting designer Robert Bryan, using a model of the set which indicates minute details of furniture and placement of light battens

**Lulu**. Opposite top left: at a Sunday technical rehearsal, lighting manager Bill McGee directs his technicians from the stage (the place of Lulu taken by an actress); opposite top right, Karan Armstrong as Lulu and Robin Leggate as the Painter enact the same scene in rehearsal, while stage manager Stella Chitty (centre, half concealed) holds Lulu's stool steady. Opposite bottom: Götz Friedrich directs Günter Reich (Dr. Schön) and Karan Armstrong (Lulu)

**Lulu**'s first night. Top: Ryszard Karczykowski (Alwa) arrives in his dressing-room and warms up his voice at the piano; Karan Armstrong becomes Lulu as she makes up; and Götz Friedrich visits the principals' dressing-rooms before the performance, right

**Lulu**. Opposite: Karan Armstrong as Lulu, in the Prologue and at the Act II murder of Dr. Schön (Günter Reich)

Below: first night audience

**Lulu**. Karan Armstrong with Erik Saedén (Schigolch);
Robin Leggate (the Negro) escapes after killing Alwa

'Madam'

**The Sleeping Beauty**. Ninette de Valois ('Madam'), rehearsing *The Sleeping Beauty* with Fiona Chadwick, Wayne Eagling and the *corps de ballet*. Three of her Auroras – Jennifer Penney, Wendy Ellis and Marguerite Porter – rehearse together, opposite top, on a stage whose birch planks receive care a few minutes before curtain-up

**The Sleeping Beauty**. Derek Deane warming up before
the Prologue. Opposite: Leslie Edwards as Cattalabutte

*Swan Lake* in dress rehearsal; Jill Gregory suggests expression while watching in the wings during *The Sleeping Beauty*; Michael Somes demonstrates a step to Rosalyn Whitten backstage during a performance

Opposite above: Anthony Dowell (Prince Siegfried) and Derek Rencher (Rothbart) in an interval during a *Swan Lake* rehearsal; below: swans and cygnets waiting on stage during a television plotting session

Below: The Royal Ballet School doctor watches in the wings as Natalia Makarova finds support from Anthony Dowell after the taxing third act of *Swan Lake*.

**The Sleeping Beauty**. Opposite: Pippa Wylde (Lilac Fairy) in the wings

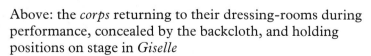
Above: the *corps* returning to their dressing-rooms during performance, concealed by the backcloth, and holding positions on stage in *Giselle*

**Mayerling.** Opposite: David Wall as Prince Rudolf, Michael Coleman as a Hungarian officer

**Swan Lake**. The triumph of the Black Swan. Wayne Eagling (Prince Siegfried), deceived by Lesley Collier (Odile) and Derek Rencher (Rothbart) and comforted by Gerd Larsen (Queen Mother), relaxes during the interval in the canteen

# BEGINNINGS

An opera production – the most expensive theatrical enterprise there is – may be generated at Covent Garden by the informal meetings of three people, a ballet by a chance impulse in the choreographer's mind, a life-giving accident.

The choice of opera springs from the enthusiasms of Sir John Tooley, Sir Colin Davis and the artistic administrator. Their meetings are frequent but they all travel constantly. Their ideas are pooled, discussed and often self-discarded. After choosing conductor and producer, they cast the singers down even to the middle-ranking and some minor roles. Little escapes them.

Over the past few years they have invited into the pit a whole roster of international conductors. The rarity of such men, and of pre-eminent tenors, gives them formidable power. So busy are they that new productions are scheduled almost five years in advance. Even a revived opera, if it is complex to cast, may be planned more than three years ahead, and the simplest must be anticipated by eighteen months.

All this needs delicate diplomacy. The matching of conductor and producer, in authority as well as temperament, the pairing of world-class singers in voice and personality – it is as subtle and unpredictable as a marriage. The most promising collusion may produce nothing, a random union become an alchemy which eludes analysis. A profound spiritual complicity between conductor, producer and singers is so rare that it borders on sorcery. Rather, for a few anxious weeks, they merge in a nervous and unplannable chemistry, inspire or irritate one another, reach an accommodation (or don't) and over a precious spate of performances produce a drama – if they succeed – whose very beauty is instinct with transience.

On this checker-board of operatic casting, the only stable factor is the presence of some twenty talented and reliable house principals, mostly maintained on a contract for fifty performances a year. No singers are more touchy when they feel that they have been overlooked in favour of foreigners; but none are more valuable for the difficult *comprimario* roles and for 'covering' the international stars; and some, like Josephine Veasey and Gwynne Howell are stars in their own right. But the days are gone when a strong resident company could dominate the repertory. Foreign contracts provide opportunities unimaginable twenty years ago, and the younger principals are mostly lured away at last to the prestigious but lonely international circuit.

The casting of the Ballet's eighty dancers is both more limited and more tense. Norman Morrice pieces together the future from a repertory of some ninety works in a bewildering iridescence of styles. He cannot plan ahead with the exactitude of the opera; the range of his dancers – their promise, their injuries – fluctuates too sharply. And it is he who commissions new choreography. Despite the expense in rehearsal time, the company keeps open house. Glen Tetley and Hans van Manen have both created ballets here in the last few years. But it is the glory and misfortune of a great opera house that it must confine itself almost wholly to established talent, and experimental ballets – the talisman for the future – find their way instead to Sadler's Wells and to the choreographic workshop founded by Leslie Edwards in 1967.

As to casting, the Ballet is dominated by its giants. Dame Ninette de Valois – redoubtable, quixotic, visionary 'Madam' – still presides over her legacy like a tutelary goddess – it is as if Sir Joshua Reynolds still walked the Royal Academy – and teaches and casts her own production of *The Sleeping Beauty*. Ashton and MacMillan, by right of contract, cast the principals for their own ballets, leaving Morrice, with his senior staff, to assemble the remaining quarter of the current repertory.

Once a week the representatives of ballet, opera, orchestra, chorus and technical staff meet to schedule the performances and to allocate rehearsal time on stage. It is politely organised civil war. For the stage is the proving ground. No studio can replace it. It is assigned for four years ahead, together with the opera and chorus rooms, and the orchestra pit. A new production may enjoy the stage for two weeks of morning rehearsals, half of them with orchestra. But the needs of musicians and stage hands, ballet and opera, grapple and collide in a labyrinthine web. The representatives' pencils hover over endlessly altered schedules. Each issue grows into a monstrous Chinese puzzle. Conductors demand extra rehearsals which the orchestra cannot give. The Ballet is accused of not planning far enough ahead. The chorus want more sessions for learning an unfamiliar score (two heavy choral operas close together produce a special pandemonium of planning). The administration manoeuvres to avoid inviting overtime. 'And does Giulini know that there's a *Freischütz* rehearsal just a few hours before his *Falstaff*?' demands the orchestra manager, probably rhetorically. 'The players need to think *Falstaff* and get their teeth into *Falstaff* – it's utterly different music. . . . This can't be done.'

The evening performances of any one opera must be delicately spaced. If they are too close together, the box office build-up is reduced and the principals' voices may be cruelly taxed. If they lie too far apart, the dramatic tension can drain away from chorus and orchestra. Nothing is consistent. *Salome* has an easily mounted set and little chorus work, but is an orchestral crucifixion. *La fanciulla del West* may be orchestrally easier but its sets are a technical nightmare.

This mosaic-like planning is necessitated by a complex schedule in which ballet and opera are interwoven more closely than anywhere outside the great theatres of the Soviet Union. Probably no great opera house in the world adheres more conscientiously to the *stagione* system, by which a production is heavily rehearsed and staged in a flush of six or seven performances over three or four weeks. The *stagione* method, common also to Italy and the United States, allows an energy and freshness to its productions which the repertory system, typical of Germany and Austria, rarely gives. A repertory house may stage an opera intermittently over many seasons, while it unnoticeably stales. Even at the Vienna Staatsoper, where new productions are generously prepared, the leading singers and conductor leave after two or three performances, and their replacements over the years are barely rehearsed at all. But at Covent Garden the *stagione* ceases a production altogether for long periods, then revitalises it with unrivalled rehearsal time; and during any ten-year span, in a huge but unequal cycle, the whole repertory is shown again.

*Top: planning committees. Above: on the set for* La fanciulla del West

Opera – whether classical or modern – enters the house by adoption, but ballet is its own created offspring. In the Royal Ballet studios at Barons Court Sir Frederick Ashton and Kenneth MacMillan are both blessed by the presence of dancers familiar to them. The studios are like a blank page: neutral arenas of creation. Their windows, closed by Venetian blinds, let in only filtered sunlight, or open on a disembodied rectangle of trees. Ashton likes the intimate Garden Studio. He shows his dancers their steps with movements still gracefully expressive. In his florid, delicately-boned face the eyes often seem faintly pained and the mouth to be savouring something ambivalent.

'The movement is still a bit slow for the music. You don't have to do this twice' – he unfurls his hands in the air – 'but it's up to you . . . if you decide to turn before the bourrée, I should. . . .'

He is choreographing a *pas de deux* for Sibley (back from retirement) and Dowell. His gaze hesitates between their feet and faces as they move. Subtle pointe-work – the beauty of the leg and foot – obsess him. With her straw-coloured hair pressed back under a white band, Sibley brings to the role an orphaned sweetness, and seems to abandon herself to the choreography like a child to a dark wood. Her bereft face flickers from Dowell to Ashton. They revise what Ashton has taught them. Dowell, in a violently-striped shirt, guides her in altered steps. He is confident and authoritative. An old enchantment glimmers in their partnership – 'We are not simply musical,' she says, 'we hear the music in the same way' – while Ashton sits silent, like a frail god watching his own creation unroll before him.

All his life he has given his dancers a hallucinatory sense that they are creating more than they are. He may transmit his desires inexactly – he will say 'Try running diagonally' or 'Be a fountain' – and so he engenders a pattern or an idea; but then he will make vital changes of rhythm or gesture, alter the *épaulement*, the poise of the head, the suppleness of the waist – and the thing will be transformed, his own.

Nothing ugly, nothing abrupt, shatters the seamless ribbon of these dances, their harmony of line, their delicate *port de bras*. They glide and fold into one another with a liquid inevitability, like figures in a Parthenaic frieze. At the root of all his work, he says, is the aesthetic impulse of love – love in its humour, its poetry, its myriad permutations. He is, perhaps, the Mozart of dance.

But between him and Kenneth MacMillan, who learnt from him while still a dancer, a dark divide opens. For Ashton the creation of beauty is a calling. For MacMillan, one suspects, such creation would be a betrayal of his own truth. He is haunted not simply by worldly decadence (*Manon*, *Mayerling*, *Playground*) but by corruption of innocence. Ashton's ballets inhabit sunlit glades of comedy or nostalgia. MacMillan's exist in a limbo of moral unease, suffering, madness. Ashton's characters are palpably loved; but with Macmillan's one is not sure – he may be hating himself through them. In him, Ashton's romantic love lurches into a whirlpool of pain and ambiguity. The abnormal and psychotic become a metaphor for man, and the very truth of him.

'Choreography for me is a kind of healing,' MacMillan says. 'I'm very obsessive, and it helps me to get rid of my obsessions. . . . My mother died when I was eleven, and I left home then, evacuated during the war. So I never had a family life after that. I had to hang on to whatever I could in the world, and I found it a very unloving place, and very overwhelming . . . it's an awful price to pay.'

From such a lesion, perhaps, derives the searing importance attached to personal relationships, and the desolate sense of betrayal at their innate obliquity, the nightmare families which erupt in *Las Hermanas* and *My Brother, My Sisters*, and the mingled fascination and disgust at erotic desire which permeates *The Invitation* or *Mayerling*. It is bitter ground – the artist exploring his hurt over and over, trying to bridge the gulf between what the child expected the world and himself to be, and what the adult discovered that they were. All this MacMillan has transmitted with extraordinary honesty.

Both he and Ashton fear beginning a ballet. MacMillan procrastinates in a deep-seated panic; Ashton used to feel physically sick each morning on the way to the underground station, and would smoke sixty cigarettes a day. The first three or four rehearsals are a wilderness for both. Yet they both begin with minds almost free of preconceived images. The calculated intentions of Antony Tudor or Hans van Manen are as alien to them as the stick-figures which used to cover the choreographic manuscripts of de Valois. They know the structure of their ballets, of course, and are steeped in the music – Ashton, especially, has sensed his dances' shape through many hours of listening. But as for the literal steps, they enter the studio with little more than an unexplored intent. Ashton, perhaps, holds in his mind some moments of visual beauty or strangeness, MacMillan a few pivotal images expressive of psychological tension. But that is all. Of their ideas they tell their dancers bewilderingly little, because they themselves are unsure what they will do. The dances and characters develop and flow out only in the act of choreography itself, and if a performer anticipated too much, he might usurp the role of creator. So the two of them – artist and instrument – proceed together in a symbiosis peculiar to dance, the one inspired by the quality of movement in the body of the other. It is a kind of faith. 'Choreo-

*Kenneth MacMillan with Monica Mason rehearsing Merle Park in* Isadora

graphy,' says Glen Tetley, 'becomes above all a response to your dancers' bodies. The most right and exciting vocabulary is the one you find there with the dancers.'

MacMillan casts his performers so well that he may sometimes release them into their roles with scarcely a word about impersonation, simply to dance as themselves. But about his steps he is specific, and he will often physically show the dancers how to move at moments when Ashton may rely on words and gestures.

The atmosphere in the studio is one of mingled dedication and humour, as among trusted friends. MacMillan sits between his choreologist, Monica Parker, and his repetiteur, Monica Mason, choreographing *Isadora* to commissioned music. Like Ashton he cannot read an orchestral score, so he must try to imagine, in the skeletal beat of the studio piano, the colour of a whole orchestration which he has never heard. Merle Park, in white woollen tights and a chiffon skirt, stands beside him with her arms folded over her (non-existent) stomach, and her hair bunched in two buns which protrude on either side of her head like the ears of a lemur. They listen to a solo as the pianist plays it through.

MacMillan says: 'This is Isadora's lament for her drowned children.' His face wears a defensive expressionlessness which is itself a kind of expression. As the music ends, he leads her to the back of the studio, and they begin.

Slowly, when the piano plays, he moves her forward by his side while his hands slide down in front of his face as if it were dripping tears. Gestures which should seem sentimental mysteriously refuse to become so. And now Park copies him, rocks her vanished children in her arms, and stoops as if taking their hands, while he watches them both in the studio mirror, giving her the movements phrase by phrase. Occasionally they stop, hunting for the right steps together, or he looses her into a moment's freedom ('Do what pleases you') and perhaps she executes a step which passes into the ballet unchanged – her own, yet somehow his too, just as everything he does is hers also – before he is guiding her once more, by the shoulders. He uses her as a writer uses pen and words, inscribes her in clauses, punctuates her, crosses her out. And the ballerina, like the words, has a not-quite-controllable life of her own, full of random nuances.

Sometimes he is running to keep up with his own inventive flow. He possesses a seemingly endless vocabulary of neo-classical imagery. When they play the solo through again, Park dances it spontaneously, singing to herself in a light, clear voice. He watches her, hesitantly pleased. Her arms furled above her head, she turns her face in grief to an imagined audience, then launches into slow, sad arabesques. Hers is a body of strange, svelte eloquence, a human violin. She has been moving athletically, almost continuously, for three quarters of an hour, but not a drop of sweat shows. Her last movement – an unfurling of her arms to either side – seems to release into death the children whom she has held; while one hand lifts further in a hint of farewell. Even in the studio, rawly created, it is a heartrending moment.

For a dancer, who has spent years following other people's steps in the classics, there is a unique delight in being the subject of a newborn ballet. In all the arts there is no more intimately shared act of creation, and some dancers, like Lynn Seymour with MacMillan, learn to anticipate the needs of their choreographer almost uncannily. ('It's intuition,' she says, 'nothing you can analyse. It's getting into his head and heart.')

Even now MacMillan tells Park very little. 'You're holding a lamp,' he says, at the start of a second dance: nothing more. So she dangles a dirty ballet slipper in lieu of a lantern. She and MacMillan stare at themselves and each other in the mirror as they advance. She

looks at him. He looks at her. She watches him; he watches her – in the mirror. 'Hold the lamp so the light is under your face.'

If there is a quintessence of MacMillan at work, it is here, moving with his dancers as though inside them, investing them with his protean emotions – 'At the end I'm always surprised by what has happened,' he says. 'I find some aspect of myself in all the characters, which is not necessarily pleasant, and something brought to light in the dancers too' – whereas the spirit of Ashton is subtly different, enkindled above all by looking: a painter perfecting his canvas, drawing an expressive line, adding a splash of light.

Rarely, MacMillan dries up, stares into nothing. Once he says: 'This music doesn't do anything for me. It sounds like *April in Paris*. I can't think of a thing to do.' He glances at the pianist. 'Play on. That may do something. . . .' Then he grows obsessed by the musical bars. 'How far are we? Have I had all my fives? . . .'

But suddenly the dance is there, finished. To a chance onlooker it would have happened almost unnoticeably, as if by accident. MacMillan has spoken sporadically and mimed a little. Park has tentatively echoed him. They have consulted, revised. Once she has done something by mistake, and he has liked and adopted it. There has apparently been nothing else. Yet here, by some sleight of hand, is a dance. It is almost as if it had assembled itself.

Many of MacMillan's most complex pieces have been effected with this mesmerising speed. Each of the four romantic *pas de deux* in *Manon* was completed in two-hour sessions over three days; those for *Mayerling* in two rehearsals each. These long duets are the core of many of his ballets, and he choreographs such important passages first, as a measure beyond which the rest of the work must not go.

As the choreography of a full evening's ballet intensifies – perhaps nine months before its first night – the preparations for an opera nine months distant are barely discernible. The producer has chosen his designer and lighting consultant, and may have found some unanimity in discussions with the conductor. But for the rest, the opera has nothing to its name but the shakey talisman of a promised cast.

Only the designer has anything tangible to show. A year before the first night, perhaps, he produces sketches of his set or a mock-up in white cardboard, and a few months later delivers detailed drafts or a finished model to the house production department. These blueprints – fantasies in wood and paper – are scrutinised by several pairs of practical eyes. The production manager and his superior, the technical director Tom Macarthur, judge how easily such prototypes may be translated into fact, and gauge their expense. They are examined by Sir John Tooley, who discusses costing with the production manager; and the chief machinist, who supervises the stage-hands, assesses them for ease of dismantling and manoeuvre.

The production design room resembles an old amusement arcade, with models set up like penny-slot machines. It is childishly exciting. They are built on an accurate but tiny scale. Their miniature cloth bars and light battens hang above a microcosmic stage with pygmy lifts. Designers follow many methods of modelling, or none. Filippo Sanjust arrives with watercolour sketches which he cuts up into Lilliputian backcloths, side-flats and solid elements. Julia Trevelyan Oman elicits her meticulous models from the depart-

*Opposite: in the flies, raising scenery*

ment's technicians. Nicholas Georgiadis produces minutely accurate mock-ups of his own.

The designer's set, ideally, is the producer's vision made palpable. It crystallises out of the conversations between them. John Schlesinger, producer of *Les Contes d'Hoffmann* conceived of Hoffmann's stories as psychotic reveries, taking place as much in the mind of the hero as in reality. So in the opera's opening Act, the dissipated Hoffmann, recalling his past *amours*, is plunged by the designer William Dudley into a backstage tavern of a kind common to the early nineteenth century. Littered with theatre props, it is a place for the manufacturing of dreams. Here Hoffmann begins his tales of recurring horror, and the episodes from his past which follow – the inventor's mansion peopled by robots, a Venetian *palazzo* washed scarlet with debauchery, the macabre house of a collector of musical instruments – are so fantastical that an audience subconsciously recognises them as the fruit of a deranged vision. Through all these delusory scenes objects from the backstage tavern where Hoffmann is seated linger like the stubborn detritus of reality. Drums and theatrical costume hampers lie about; a clown's mask loiters mocking on a wall. The ghoulish double-bass cases which seem spectrally alive in the house of the instrument-collector are redolent of a backstage orchestra mezzanine, and for each exotic setting the tavern's stairs split and reassemble yet remain dimly reminiscent of their origin. Such leftovers, like the flotsam around a drowning man, impart an insidious feeling that every scene is coloured by the voice of Hoffmann, and that perhaps, after all, these dramas are no more than the ramblings of a ruined mind.

Similarly, it was a chance remark to his designer by the producer Götz Friedrich which engendered the pervasive motif for *Lulu*. The characters in this heartless opera, he felt, were the prisoners of their own passions – creatures in a menagerie (he talks, characteristically, of 'the world prison'). So Timothy O'Brien designed a set like the ring of a claustrophobic animal circus. Its central acting area was small and harshly isolated (the stage lifts sunk around it). A chance spectator might creep close to it – on tiptoe, as it were – and witness the self-blinded depravity within. Its protagonists reached the ring by cage-like corridors. Sometimes they beat impotently on the bars, sometimes they were allowed to enter. They were, in either case, trapped. And within this arena the progress of Lulu was defined in cruel trajectory by the state of her dress – from respectable, to luxuriously fashionable, to the pathos of the prostitute. Only with her murder by Jack the Ripper – the murder which she half desires – is the cage broken apart. Then, as Jack walks away, two 24-foot-high doors open on a column of light. There is a sudden sense of air and space, and something – separate from the woman lying in her blood – seems to fly out into the day.

Sets like these become themselves compulsive protagonists in the drama; but others, such as those for *Lohengrin* and Britten's *Peter Grimes*, achieve their power by a reductive simplicity. The very bareness of the setting for *Peter Grimes*, evoking empty seascapes and sky, throws emphasis on the people who inhabit it – their trade, their human complexity, their brutal cohesion. 'I think it was when we stood by the edge of the sea at Aldeburgh,' says its co-designer O'Brien, 'that we had an idea of something more elemental than we'd supposed, and imagined a simplified stage where we could present a community in all its diversity, and ask an audience to look into it.'

Such creative complicity between designer and producer takes place in ballet between designer and choreographer. A comment by MacMillan – that he envisaged Act I of

*Manon* inhabited by beggars – awoke in Nicholas Georgiadis an old obsession about contrasted opulence and squalour ('I find it a very piquant thing') and so gave birth to the tattered backdrops and side-flats which pervade even the ballet's most luxurious episodes with a continuing threat of poverty. The problem peculiar to staging ballet – the imposed vacuum of the central dancing area – has fascinated designers like Georgiadis and Barry Kay since the early 1960s, when dance was still produced in little more than painted scenery and backcloths. From such thin friezes, Kay plucks the performers into three-dimensional space. His sets are solidly constructed. Above the stage's obligatory void he carves the air with a compensatory landscape – the translucent whorls of parchment in *Anastasia*, the inflated tree of *Solitaire*.

Georgiadis is teased by the possibilities of a set – forced into such constrictions – expressing itself by a powerful visual shorthand. In *Mayerling*, for instance, the apartment of the Empress Elisabeth is evoked by a few dress-stands; they are the irreducible symbol both of her boudoir and of her vanity. Yet Georgiadis does not at first conceive his productions with this economy at all. He envisages them more as film shots – but flat, pictorial – then finds his essential images and retreats a little from naturalism altogether. This reputedly realistic designer feels that ballet in a totally realistic set is misplaced ('In real life people don't do arabesques'). Besides, the topography of the empty stage forbids it. So in *Mayerling* the dark surrounding gauzes are no more true to life than the tatters of *Manon*. Only its isolated furniture is palpably realistic. And the angels which brood over the mausoleum in *Romeo and Juliet* – mere parodies of Florentine bas-relief – invoke the weight of death by their very disproportion.

The play of fantasy, from the romantically traditional designs of Peter Farmer to Ian Spurling's dizzying ranks of reflectors for *The Seven Deadly Sins*, has occupied ballet design more exclusively than that of opera. Even the costumes for opera indulge a greater realism. For durability, they are often better made than everyday clothes, yet their natural effect is generally the result of artifice, and the intentions behind them vary. They may be conceived simply (or subtly) to express personality; or to heighten the dramatic episodes in which the characters act; they may underline social standing as those for *Lulu* do; or reflect a culture, like Michael Stennett's in *Alceste*.

David Walker's *Don Giovanni* costumes were conceived as expressions of situation. So in the first Act the pallor of Donna Anna's nightdress – the lightest tone on stage – stresses her near-violated virginity, and isolates her. Its agitating whiteness is echoed only in the shirt of her murdered father, and by two sacerdotal statues which hover on the colonnade high above. The Don's costumes, on the other hand, intensify between Acts from the plum-coloured reticence of a black-slashed doublet and black boots to the defiant crimson and gold in which he goes to his damnation; whereas the anger of Donna Elvira's entrance is enhanced by Walker's choice of material for her riding-habit – a green-blue velvet which shimmers and smoulders as she strides about.

But some operas seem above all to demand the evocation of a culture. For *Alceste* the spacious simplicity of Gluck's music suggested to Michael Stennett and to his producer John Copley a slow, processional quality, the dignity of the ancient Greek world as the eighteenth century conceived it. So Stennett sought for costumes which would transmit the clarity and strength of Hellenic sculpture. He devised them in materials veined and mottled like marble, or redolent of long-buried bronze, or verdigris, and had lengths of rope sewn into the fabric so that it fell in marmoreal folds like those of ancient statuary.

Thus the chorus of *Alceste* submerged its variety to become figures in a Greek landscape.

*Les Contes d'Hoffmann* achieved precisely the opposite. One and a half years before its opening night, after consultation with Schlesinger and Dudley, the designer Maria Björnson devised more than three hundred and twenty costumes. After studying photographs of the whole cast, including a chorus of seventy-five, she invented a character around each one and clothed him accordingly. She spent six weeks merely sketching the designs. One person could have been employed for two months sewing on the buttons alone. During fifty fittings a day the singers and costumiers spilt out of the wardrobe department's two tiny fitting-rooms – barely adequate for a provincial repertory theatre – and into the wig department, the wardrobe director's office and even the lavatories, and crammed into the backstage dressing-rooms five at a time.

The employees of the wardrobe department, which occupies the top storey of '45', have been praised by several international designers as more enthusiastic and involved than those of any other great opera house. In its pattern room, whose walls are lichened with samples, the costume supervisors for ballet and opera confabulate with designers among harlequin scatterings of satin and lace. The choosing of fabrics is a difficult and exhilarating time. They are bought *en masse* from many different companies, often from France, Germany or Switzerland, but since their colours can rarely match those conceived by the designer, they are dyed again in the department's vats.

Each costume is individually cut. The wardrobe director selects the projects best suited to the department's eight workrooms, and assigns the rest to outside contractors who may work almost full-time for the house. The measurements of every singer and dancer employed – principals, chorus, *corps* – are kept on file, or have been obtained by telephone calls to agents and other opera houses. It is a prodigious task.

Some three months before dress rehearsal, the designer briefs his cutters on style, proportion, shape. In rooms full of purring sewing-machines and warm laundry smells they start to snip out rough patterns in calico, which they pin on dress-stands to gauge the costume's form. As a production advances, the rooms fill up with half-materialised ghosts – a travelling-cloak assembled alone on one dress-stand, seventeenth-century elbow-sleeves blooming disembodied on another – all tacked up to await a first fitting, their seams and hems lightly stitched.

Such tailored costumes emerge stronger and more emphatic than everyday clothes. Their materials are enduring and sometimes, for singers, cruelly heavy. Bodices are lined and often boned. Silk replaces taffeta, which fades too quickly and deadens in stage-light. Nothing is skimped. By 1981 some opera costumes, with their attendant shoes and jewellery, cost almost five hundred pounds. The big auditorium swallows detail, so that lace and braid trimmings have to be crudely elevated and thickened. Everything is larger than life. New costumes, which might appear bland on stage, are touched up like portraits in the dye shop, their folds sprayed dark, and the areas around belts and lapels modulated by false shading.

The bodies of singers and dancers are a costumier's maze of sensitive and neutral zones. The singer's ribs and throat are especially susceptible. Janet Baker, for instance, cannot bear a costume to touch her neck; and a high woollen collar in the *Ring* created such a dead sound-box behind Donald McIntyre's head that he had to adjust his hearing by sticking chewing-gum behind his ears. Helmets and masks are loathed; and tunics which drag on the back and shoulders can constrict the chest and cause violently aching ribs. Some singers want the diaphragm tightly enclosed; they need the sensation of breathing against something. Others prefer it free. Ileana Cotrubas likes costumes which barely seem to touch her, whereas Eda Moser, who succeeded to her role in *Les Contes d'Hoffmann*, asked for the same dress to be drawn in skin tight. The members of the chorus have idiosyncracies of their own. One is hypersensitive to wool against her skin (so her costumes are specially lined); another breaks out in rashes at the touch of horsehair, another on contact with black dye. The baritone Thomas Allen, who is allergic to feathers (they make him sneeze), had to play Papageno in plumage cut out of organza.

Light fabrics, lightly lined – silks, cottons, airy woollens – are ideal. But they are not always possible. The men in *Lohengrin* dress in twenty-five metres each of heavy woollens. And velvets, which are hot to wear, yet look beautiful under stage lights.

Singers' sizes fluctuate. Occasionally the chorus is subjected to massive remeasurements, which are scarcely needed for the dancers. The recurring challenge is to make sopranos appear slender and tenors tall. Elongating cloaks and baldricks, dresses whose vertical lines taper to the waist, blocked shoes, false-seamed boots which are elevated inside – the ingenuities are legion; and costumes are often sprayed darker under the shoulders and down the sides, so that the silhouette is shaded away.

Clothes for the Ballet are lighter, less structured. But each new costume has a future history of partnership or isolation as specific as a person's. In new choreography, the designer and supervisor have to acquaint themselves with these numberless futures – to modify a skirt, perhaps, if it is worn in an acrobatic *pas de deux*, or to guard against slippery fabrics for difficult lifts. The dancer's shape changes slowly, if at all. Only after the August holiday does the wardrobe staff expect aberrant measurements: men's shoulder muscles dwindled, jackets wrinkled up by fatter bottoms, girls' waists thickened through slacker sinews.

The need, above all, is for unrestricted movement and expressive silhouette. As with a singer, the rib-cage must be freed for breathing; but the vital measurement is that between shoulder and crutch – a body length as individual as a fingerprint. Extra folds inserted beneath the armpits ensure that the costume does not lift when the arms do. Yet for these extended postures low-necked dresses must be cut long enough to retain the girls' breasts. Risqué bodices are sometimes saved from scandal by flesh-coloured nets stretched over the bosom, and a ballerina's fish-dives and somersaults display knickers of a different colour from her flesh-white stockings, to avoid the illusion of nakedness. But for her partner, the axis of her body is the waist, and her costume is always set on a waistband – often an inner basque from which the skirt falls in three or four layers to emphasise her slenderness. Yet her period costume is often an illusion. The voluminous bustles in *Mayerling*, for instance, flow over frames parted in the centre so that the dancer's leg can still lift ninety degrees. For *Anastasia* the hobble skirts – a balletic impossibility – are furnished with hidden overlaps, so that the leg can both stretch and be perfectly covered.

The designer's choice of textile is vital. Different fabrics possess different qualities of movement. Even colours change their strength in motion – blue grows more powerful, yellow dims. Light, washable materials are favourites — silks and voils (the most tweedy textures can be simulated by raw silk.) But the durability of fabrics is always on trial. The average net tutu, unless it is dyed, remains so strong that it will last fifty performances in the *corps* of *Swan Lake*, whereas chiffon, although mesmerising, is miserably frail – the heroine's nightdress in *Romeo and Juliet* grows irreparably tattered after only seven or eight performances.

Many costumes, after their tailoring is complete, are returned to the dyeing room, whose steamy vats, sinister spraying booth and dyes simmering in chamber-pots all create a feel of homely witchcraft. Here costumes are patterned by hand or block or silk screen printing. Others, finished and fine, are systematically broken down to appear old. This creative destruction is left to the ingenuity of the dyeing supervisor. Pristine suits are soaked underwater then hung up in saddening rows, their fabric faded here and there with unobtrusive spraying, their weighted pockets sagging into Chaplinesque neglect. The ravaged body-stockings for *Gloria* were sprayed over streaks of applied plastic to produce an effect almost of peeling flesh. The cowboy jeans in *La fanciulla del West*, bought brand new, were pinned into folds, bleached pale and unpinned again to show world-weary creases around the crutch. But these are nothing compared to the careful havoc wrought on costumes for the down-and-out. They are torn with cheese-graters, shredded by wire brushes, ripped with Stanley knives. Finally a home-made emulsion of sawdust and glue, compounded with stray wisps of sacking collected by the supervisor in her holiday moments, is thrown against the costumes to simulate plastered mud.

The wardrobe rooms are surrounded by satellites: jewellery, wigs, millinery. Ballet headgear inclines to close-fitting ornament – balletomanes traditionally love the small, jewelled head of the dancer – and hats have to be fiercely secured by elastic and hair-grips pushed through steel or cotton loops. But the multiform operatic headdresses are built up until they are all but indestructible. Their inner fabrics thicken into two layers instead of the usual one; stiffening glue is extra powerful. Everyday headgear is gossamer compared to these steely cloches and bonnets and imperishable tricornes; the top hats are little more collapsible than rocks. But all this finery must leave the jaws and ears free. Wide-brimmed hats distort sound; so may the cheek-bands of helmets or any element which hugs the face in front; and cotton cowls grate against the ears unless modified by gauze.

Headwear sizes depend on wig sizes. The opera house owns – astonishingly – thirty thousand wigs; but every piece must look so natural, so individual, that ten wig-makers work full-time on creating new ones. These are all made from human hair, in which a shadowy trade exists out of Hong Kong and the Eastern Bloc. The straight, black Asiatic hair, bleached and dyed to different colours, is coarse enough to hold its shape well after setting, but eventually straightens on the humid stage; whereas the finer Caucasian hair loses its style faster, but may be naturally curly. The wig-maker's task is minute as insects' work. An average piece takes seven days to complete. Massed over a fine net around the hairline and down the parting, every hair is stitched in individually with a knotting-hook, and even at the back, where the tresses are riveted in tiny clumps, the shades have been delicately mixed on a hackle to give them the faintly varied lustre of a living coiffure.

In performance the artist's own hair is curled to the shape of the head, flattened in a stocking, then the wig pinned over it and secured to the forehead by a few streaks of spirit gum. Beards and moustaches are stuck firmly against sweating, but tiny gaps are left on the most mobile and sensitive parts of the face – under the nostrils, around the mouth-corners – to be concealed by drifts of surrounding moustache. Hardest of all to disguise are the plastic pates which mimic baldness. These, too, are the province of the wigmaster on performance nights. He sets them as near to the hairline as possible (movement

Facets of the wardrobe: creating jewellery, dressmaking, storage of fabrics, and the armoury work benches

decreases higher up the head) and blends them to the forehead by a flow of makeup which attempts to reproduce the tones and imperfections – even the broken blood vessels – of the individual skin. Nothing, perhaps, is more difficult to imitate than the effect of living hair, except none at all.

Down the passage from the wig department, with its hint of necrophilia and *haute couture*, the little jewellery workshop winks and corruscates with false gems, bracelets, wings, ribbons, spiked and pearl-hung diadems. Everything glitters and trembles in an air scented with paint and acetone. It is like a bazaar or a crazy junk shop filled with the collection of a madman or genius. Its walls are invisible for pots of glass bijouterie, photographs of ballerinas, gold lace, post-cards of other people's holidays, goat-masks for *Sylvia* (never used), plastic pearls. One day the floor-space may be monopolised by tables strewn with paste rubies, the next by a dress-stand girded with a chain-hung corslet for *Salome* – a punk bikini.

As in other departments, there is an utter lack of precedent. One day will demand bangles for *Die Fledermaus*, the next a black and silver spider's claw for *Les Contes d'Hoffmann*. The three jewellery makers extrapolate freely from the usually tenuous sketches of the designer. Their artefacts are improvised out of malleable cardboard, wire framing and metallic braid, then touched up with enamel paints mixed in the compartments of old egg-boxes. Jewels themselves are reproduced with the simplest of materials – crumpled scraps of baking-foil coated with warm cellulose, then coloured. Only the principal dancers and singers enjoy the luxury of faceted crystal gems.

Some singers say that if the head and feet are well dressed, they can tolerate anything. The shoe is security. Its obligatory rubber soles are soft and gripping on the stage. For opera principals, shoes are made to measure in two weeks, but can be rushed together within forty-eight hours during emergency. The chorus is fed by a huge stock of women's court shoes and men's elastic-sided boots, and each member is issued with four personal pairs – peasant suedes for such operas as *Simon Boccanegra*, black leather character shoes, *Aida*-style sandals, and general purpose footwear for *Otello* or *La Bohème*.

Every pair of ballet shoes is individually made for its dancer (almost all by Freed). Iron shelves in the depths of the house, and wicker skips and hampers in '51' overflow with character footwear and with the men's soft-toe shoes in leather or canvas (the one supple, the other cool) and include a little stock for the only male role danced on pointe – the asinine Bottom in Ashton's *The Dream*; while the girls' pink satin pointe shoes – ranging from size seven down to two-and-a-half – are stacked in a monastic sanctuary near the *corps* dressing-rooms.

The ballet slipper is the symbol of the profession, a part of its mystique. Its spine is a thick cardboard insole, its sides stiffened by paste high up in the lining; a soft leather sole completes it. But dancers spend hours preparing these shoes to their special needs. They slice the slippery satin from the pointe, batter the 'clonk' out of the papier-mâché head, squeeze and waggle the cardboard and shave away the edges of the sole for greater elasticity. The stronger the dancer, the more pliable and weak she may allow her shoe to be. It becomes like a skin of her foot. She blends it to the line of her leg by dulling its shine in stage makeup and she sews on its ribbons herself.

A dancer may preserve a favourite pair of shoes by constant varnishing, but their life is

*Les Contes d'Hoffmann. In the chorus changing room, before Act II*

never long. The opera house makes an allowance of twelve pairs a month to each principal, ten to every member of the *corps*. A single tough rehearsal can dispose of a pair in little more than an hour, and the heroine of *Swan Lake* may run through three in an evening, so that on a performance night the shoes' supervisor does not leave her alcove of slippers until the last Act is on stage.

Still deeper than this den of pink satin, in one of the near-subterranean corridors beneath the auditorium, is a vault whose door is sunk in iron and whose vents have been sealed up by police order. The house firemen have pass keys to every room except this one. Closed in an airless dark, it holds the core of the house armoury. Guns and swords glimmer in double phalanxes along its walls. Giant Wagnerian shields and spears, battle-maces and yataghans, ceremonial Russian axes, Elizabethan halberds, matchlocks, claymores, cutlasses are all stacked like terrible and ill-matched regiments one opposite the other in a battle-array transcending time. Many of them are genuine. The house armoury was started in the late 1950s, when antique arms could still be bought for a few pounds each. It is unique in British theatre. Eighty original cavalry spears stand cheek by jowl with a hundred and twenty 1860 rifles, some of whose lock-plates are stamped 'East India Company' or 'Tower of London' (but nobody knows how they came here). Their ugly habits are not always cured by being on stage. A few of the muskets have lost their antique value – they were adapted after an accident in the execution scene of *Tosca*; and one night a sword-fight in *Romeo and Juliet* sent foot-long splinters flying through the orchestra among jittery players and musical instruments insured for up to many thousands of pounds each.

The armoury staff undertake welding repairs and make scabbards, baldricks and hilts. Blades are forged outside the house, but from a stock of over five hundred swords the armourers pirate the pommel of one, the hilt of another, and so confect new weapons at a designer's request. Their workrooms high in the house reek of leather and iron filings, and are stuffed with arms in a jumble of centuries as demented as that of their basement arsenal. Half a dozen 1620 bilboes and sixty Waterloo sabres line up with Indian tribal scimitars and a Russian shashka – an evil sliver of light. With these stand instruments of pure theatre. Wotan's broadsword from the *Ring* cycle releases a broken chunk of blade by a trick mechanism in the hilt. And here is the satanic armament of the Queen of the Night's maidens – a Perspex sword illumined by internal flashbulbs for the slaughter of the serpent in *Die Zauberflöte*.

Yet all these accoutrements – arms, jewellery, wigs, the costumes themselves – are being assembled for opera stars who may be absent until a month before the first night. Only the British singers – probably house principals – have been preparing their roles with the Covent Garden repetiteurs. Six months in advance, perhaps, the two corridors of studios in '45' and '51' send up a muffled antiphony of soprano and baritone, Verdi and Strauss. Twelve or thirteen different operas may mingle and contradict one another in the passageways in a single day, and may be joined (at least in the imagination) by Wagnerian thunderings where the conductor Reginald Goodall gives lessons in a private Valhalla high up behind the amphitheatre.

The twelve house repetiteurs divide into specialists of German and Italian repertory. They play the piano at rehearsals, act as prompters in performances and conduct the

*Les Contes d'Hoffmann. Chorus, Act I*

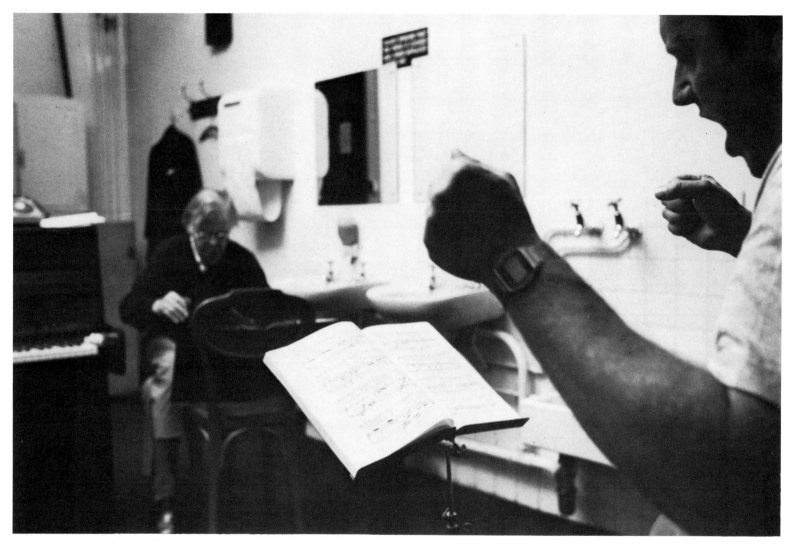

Reginald Goodall coaching Gwynne Howell in his studio, an old washroom behind the amphitheatre. Repetiteur Nina Walker, above, prompting a stage rehearsal

offstage bands. But above all they develop musical interpretation with the soloists in these Covent Garden studios.

'Never start singing the phrase without thinking the whole sentence – just as if it's a new thought' – it is the recurring demand of the repetiteur Nina Walker as she coaches a powerful forty-year-old bass. 'The whole breath process is dependent on the thought process. If you know what you're going to sing, you won't run out of breath in the wrong place . . .'

He faces her in the curve of the piano, huge and uncertain. Like many singers, he has come late to the profession. She plays the piano in the repetiteur's way, miming the opulence and breadth of an orchestra by a strong harmonic and rhythmic bass, less detail in the treble. The piano and voice sound immense together in the low-ceilinged room. She tries to take him back in spirit to the libretto, to return to the words which faced Verdi before he composed the music, to retrace the creative process. 'When you go home, walk around your room reading out the sentences. Learn the thought processes. Then shape the phrase. If you do this you'll follow what Verdi did.'

He sings again. The voice starts to glow. His knees bend a little and he clasps his hands in front of him, weaving and unlacing their fingers. Occasionally she shouts at him over the piano: 'Sing what you *think*. . . . Don't bring the voice out on its own – it's bland, it means nothing. . . . Don't break the word in the middle, that's not Verdi . . .'

Sometimes, in quiet moments, the sound from a neighbouring studio penetrates this one: Stuart Burrows rehearsing *Così fan tutte*. Projected with shining accuracy into the bare room, where the opera house carpet dribbles in faded strips and iron girders show across the ceiling, the patrician voice falls on the ear like a benediction – a touchstone of the possible.

**Isadora.** Opposite: Kenneth MacMillan choreographing with Judith Howe, Derek Rencher and Merle Park, and the actress Mary Miller. Right: Merle Park and Julian Hosking. Below: MacMillan with Stephen Jefferies, Graham Fletcher and Sally Inkin

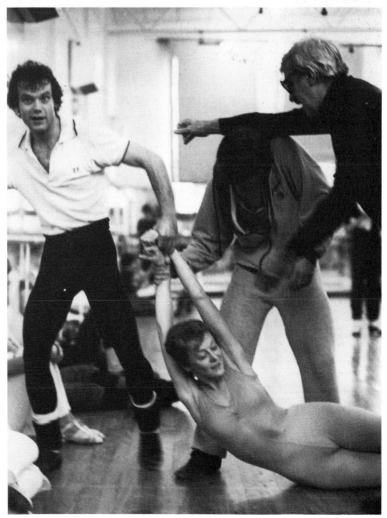

**Isadora.** Above: stage manager Keith Gray, designer Barry Kay (centre) and Kenneth MacMillan at the production desk during a session for lighting the sets. Right: composer Richard Rodney Bennett, conductor Barry Wordsworth (centre) and Kenneth MacMillan in discussion after stage rehearsal

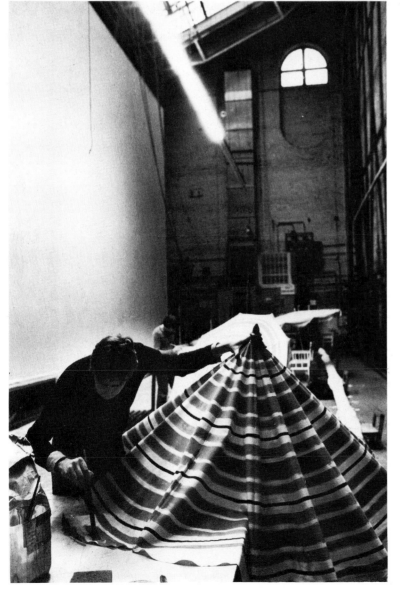

**Isadora** in production. Dressmaking in a workshop hung with newly-made tutus; colouring a sunshade in the paint frame above the stage; spraying a gramophone horn in the props workshops

**Isadora's** first night. Kenneth MacMillan in the wings;
Merle Park prepares in a dressing-room hung with
telegrams; and David Wall, prevented by injury from
dancing the leading male role, embraces MacMillan after
the performance

Laura Connor as Loie Fuller, Monica Mason as Nursey

**Les Contes d'Hoffmann.** Producer John Schlesinger, at a rehearsal in the Crush Bar, directs Nicola Ghiuselev (Dr. Miracle), and Gwynne Howell (Crespel), for their confrontation in Act III

**Les Contes d'Hoffmann**. At the first costume fittings designer Maria Björnson, with wardrobe staff and dressmakers, assembles basted costumes on Placido Domingo, left, on Sir Geraint Evans, right, and on two members of the chorus

**Les Contes d'Hoffmann**. Maria Björnson, exhausted during the fitting of over 300 costumes, sits in the millinery department, while work continues on trimmings in the dressmaking rooms, on hat fittings and wig adjustments.

Opposite: John Schlesinger directs a rehearsal of *Les Contes d'Hoffmann*, with conductor Georges Prêtre (left) and assistant producer Richard Gregson (right); and assesses the stage set for Act I

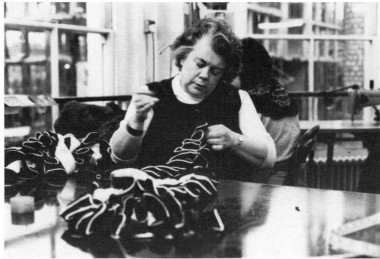

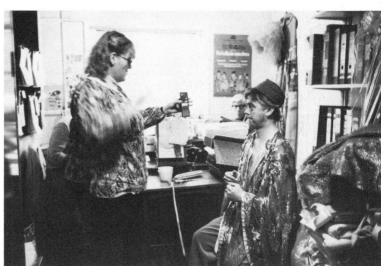

**Les Contes d'Hoffmann**. Opposite: in the intervals. The men's chorus changing and washing, while irreverent principals peer from the old dressing-rooms

A *Sitzprobe* of *Les Contes d'Hoffmann*. The chorus in the auditorium conducted by Georges Prêtre from the pit, with the principals seated on stage

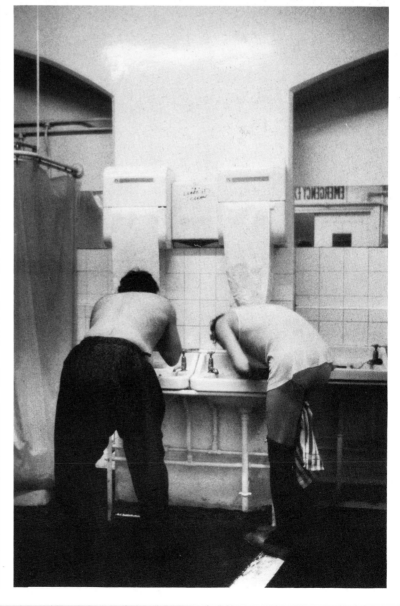

**Les Contes d'Hoffmann**. Robert Tear as Spalanzani, winding up his harp, which is operated through a cable by an electrician and stage manager (second and third from right) in the wings. Fitted with three tiny interior motors, it 'accompanies' the aria of the mechanical doll Olympia, sung by Luciana Serra

Opposite: Placido Domingo as Hoffmann, Geraint Evans as Coppélius, exposing the mechanical doll

**Les Contes d'Hoffmann**, Act II. Members of the chorus

Les Contes d'Hoffmann: interludes. A chorus member
dozes on stage before curtain-up for Act II. The wardrobe
master in the wings sews up a two-foot tear in Placido
Domingo's trousers a few minutes before he returns to the
stage as Hoffmann

Opposite: Act III, Ileana Cotrubas as Antonia sings to her
death

Auditions for principal roles, which are held on stage, are attended by Sir Colin Davis, with the artistic administrator, music staff and consultants, and produce numerous impromptu meetings afterwards

**Madama Butterfly.** Lowered beneath the sets on one of the huge stage elevators, the assistant chorus master, left, watches the conductor on a closed-circuit television and cues the entrance of Raina Kabaivanska (Cio-Cio-San). Below, he conducts the offstage female chorus after her denunciation by the Bonze, sung by Richard Van Allan, bottom.

**Romeo and Juliet.** Gerd Larsen as the Nurse, opposite. Below, top row, rehearsing with Michael Coleman, Michael Batchelor and Lesley Collier (Juliet). Her padded costume, assembled by her dresser, centre, lends her a voluminous dignity. She impresses on the Juliet of Gelsey Kirkland, bottom left, or of Merle Park, bottom right, that the girl's childhood is over

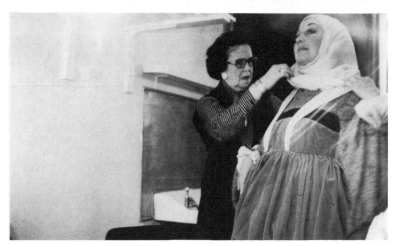

**Romeo and Juliet**. Opposite: stage hands hoover the floorcloth before Act II; and Wendy Ellis talks with the conductor, Emanuel Young, before Act III
Above: the formidable Lord Capulet of Michael Somes commands Juliet (Gelsey Kirkland) to marry Paris. Below: Derek Rencher as Paris, Merle Park as Juliet

**Romeo and Juliet**: a diversity of Juliets. Gelsey Kirkland, top, running to Friar Lawrence's cell; Lesley Collier, above, relinquishing Romeo at dawn; Merle Park, right, with Wayne Eagling and the wardrobe staff, in an interval before curtain-up

Moments after performance. Kenneth MacMillan with Wendy Ellis, top; Anthony Dowell at curtain call, left; HRH Prince Andrew with Lesley Collier and Wayne Eagling, above

# IN THE STUDIO

The melancholy experienced after a first rush of creation is an artist's commonplace. Ashton is never happy until a ballet is complete, and is then only relieved. MacMillan grows deeply despondent towards the middle of a work, and already thinks of its audience with dread. Six weeks before the first night, perhaps, he is choreographing his last pieces, probably on the *corps*. These are moments which can baffle him. After many hours, *corps*-work for both *The Rite of Spring* and for *Gloria*, he abandoned everything he had done and began again – a bitter decision for dances created in the sweat of others. To him a *corps* – a crowd – is a little meaningless or threatening. His instinct is to break it into its human fractions, otherwise he cannot speak through it.

As he moves the dancers for a *pas de six*, he is more precise with them than with the principals. 'Do a turned-in *pas de chat* . . . go forward on pointe . . . the head should be downstage . . .' The leading girl copies him; the rest copy her, and a trio of understudies shadows them all behind. Once he groups them physically with his hands in a fleeting but pivotal statement. Often he stares at his reflection in the mirror, where his own body may temporarily seem as separate from him as theirs, while they wait to be told what to do.

The girls are very different. Some of their faces are lit and soft, others formal, almost depleted. It is as if years of ferocious training, which subdues the natural line of their dancing into a near-perfect *corps*, leaves its constraint on all but the strongest. Sometimes MacMillan tacitly looks to one of them for a lead. Then he sets them moving in a pastiche Greek dance. They become like dolls twirling on the lid of a musical box to a dry tinkle: something discovered in an attic. He demonstrates their movements phrase by phrase. They weave complex patterns, grow confused, giggle and bump into one another. From time to time they start from the beginning, miming in slow motion, and end up in a statuesque and changing garland, like figures on a classical vase.

He changes little in revision. Whole sessions will go by in which he watches rather than speaks. Unlike Ashton, who touches in colours and inflections on the broad canvas of his original, MacMillan creates his movements almost whole. Occasionally, in rehearsal, a step is confused or forgotten, fails to fit the music. Then he appeals to the choreologist sitting beside him – she has annotated his original – and the dancers try again; or Monica Mason, the mediatrix between his mind and their bodies, shows them the steps. Just as a singer can never truly hear his own voice, so a dancer never really sees himself. 'Your feet are moving wrong, they look too lyrical,' MacMillan tells Park in a tense *pas de deux*. 'They look like butterfly feet. I want something more *cruel*.' And once he calls out: 'You do that too long, it's not an interesting step!' as if it were hers rather than his. And as he does so, it becomes apparent that he considers her his emanation: it is an act of self-criticism.

At about this time, too, the full-scale rehearsals begin, first Act by Act, then the ballet complete. Taking the largest studio lengthwise, to duplicate the Covent Garden stage, the dancers prepare to rehearse in a barrage of critical stares. MacMillan in dark glasses, de Valois looking inscrutable, Mason, two choreologists, a ballet master, the stage manager Keith Gray – they are perched in a familiar but needle-eyed line, cradling its Benesh notation, jotting memoranda. The dancers sit on the floor round three walls of the studio. They whisper together. Their ages range between forty-three and eighteen, but for the moment they all seem conflated into unaging students. Above their clasped arms and drawn-up knees, their disciplined multitude of eyes fills the dance-space with a level inquisition.

MacMillan waits to begin, his arms folded, his expression authoritative in a helmet of grey-black hair. But in fact, he's terrified. He is facing the whole company with a ballet still raw and unjoined, and his dancers cannot know what is polished, what unresolved. Compared to the straight theatre, rehearsals have been few and sporadic. There is an everlasting lack of time. So at first everything falls apart, and in the close studio the illusion of lightness is gone. The dancers labour to retrieve steps forgotten over long intervals. Uncertain, they dance with a ragged physical strain, faces flushed. The delicate touches are everywhere mislaid. The whole work has lost its pristine energy and seems to have faded into a skeleton of what was once created. Some of the dancers forget their steps altogether and stop in exasperation. The choreologists direct them with gestures and counting. Complicated *pas de deux* fail; the partners try different solutions between them, while MacMillan advises, willing to change his steps if the effect emerges the same.

Merle Park and Stephen Jefferies attempt a series of formidably difficult lifts. 'I've been practising this one with my dog,' says Jefferies. Park moans softly to herself. 'At least it has four legs.'

It seems as if the very stuff of *Isadora* has to be rediscovered: its mingled parody and pathos, MacMillan's long obsession with isolation, with the lost. And suddenly there is something touching in this very private man committing his pain to the public scrutiny.

Only Park's solos – the dances of lamentation, the lantern dance – seem lissome and effortless. To perform a big role fully for the first time, unsure of its tax on stamina, carries a unique anxiety. And a dancer is never on such trial as she is here, circled by the cross-fire of sixty others in the naked studio. She moves in a wan, neutral light. Every step is exposed. The surrounding faces are more critical, and more mercilessly present, than those in a darkened auditorium. But Park seems to dance without muscle, by a gift of will. Like a musical singer spurning the literal note values, she caresses the choreographic phrase, softening one step, stressing another, letting them speak. MacMillan removes his dark glasses; his only sign of nervousness is a compulsive chewing. As Park finishes, her fellow-dancers break into spontaneous applause, and he gets up and encloses her face affectionately in his hands.

Meanwhile the second-cast Isadora, Sandra Conley, starved of rehearsals, watches and feels separate, unable to experience the role in her own body. It still belongs only to Park.

But one by one these full rehearsals gather strength. Slowly the ballet is rediscovered, is elaborated and begins to flow. MacMillan forges theatrical links between its episodes. The burden or delight of such stage-craft falls to him (usually there is no producer for ballet) and to his more enterprising dancers, who develop mise-en-scène between themselves. Props appear: a couch, some plastic lilies. And Conley's Isadora develops and separates from Park's, growing distraught and vulnerable against the other's predatory sadness.

As time presses, observers thicken in the studio: Norman Morrice, Richard Rodney Bennett the music's composer, and Ashley Lawrence, the Royal Ballet's music director. Keith Gray tapes out the floor to indicate the placement of scenery, and scans the last rehearsals to learn his cues. The conductor Barry Wordsworth gauges where to heighten and where to integrate the piano's percussive theme – the dancer's guideline – into the orchestral texture which will soon replace piano altogether.

Meanwhile Barry Kay, the designer, seated between MacMillan and the lighting consultant, is imagining the performers in his costumes. A finished dance may suggest to him a mood different than it did in mere discussion, or a sequence of steps clarify some element of dress. So he has remained flexible until this late moment and now sketches quietly on the back of a design sheet: changes of hairstyle, notes on fabrics, on an unexpected conjuncture of soloists which sets him worrying about colour clashes. The lighting consultant talks with him and with MacMillan, listening to the music's mood, and scribbles down provisional ideas: 'Scene 4: maybe dull, grey light . . . very cold, practical . . . dissolve to warm interior. . . .'

The ballet moves towards stage rehearsal in a security unknown to opera. The dancer is an instrument tuned fine and exclusive to his calling, and the company is his surrogate family; but singers are more independent and volatile. At worst the star system sheds a megalomaniac pall over the whole profession. Many of its finest dramas happen offstage. But at best the visiting principals bring to a production not only vocal beauty but a musical insight and dedication which lifts and energises the whole work. Their rehearsals are fiercely concentrated. Even for a new production they may begin a mere five weeks

*John Tooley with the artistic administrator, Helga Schmidt*

IN THE STUDIO

before its first night – and this is generous compared to many other houses.

The assembled cast wastes no time. Handshakes, some practical enquiries, a little joking – and they launch into the music. In Sir Colin Davis's opera house suite – small, grey-carpeted rooms with one grand piano – the principals for *Don Giovanni* sit in little blue-upholstered chairs with their scores on their knees. Ruggero Raimondi, Gundula Janowitz, Kiri te Kanawa, Stuart Burrows, Gwynne Howell – the cast sings through the opera all morning and afternoon while Davis points up a rhythm here, a syllable there, in the eternal quest for new meaning, the return to the words. ('The beautiful things in Mozart are by the way,' he says. 'You aim at making dramatic exchanges. They may just happen to be rather beautiful.')

The next day they are all in a stage-wide rehearsal studio with the producer Peter Wood. Opposite them, behind a piano and a barrage of tables littered with schedules and libretti, the assistant producers, stage management and music staff watch and annotate. A model of the future set stands nearby, but its palace colonnades and magisterial stairway are represented on the studio floor only by scattered chairs and coloured tapes. Under the stress of time and of one another, a precarious happiness develops among the singers. The recitative fascinates and challenges them. With Wood and Davis, they take it apart and reassemble it in a burst of enthusiasm and discovery, as if they had never sung it before. Davis stands in front of them, impassioned by the music, eliciting their exchanges with curling gestures of his hands, seeking precision and variety. Beside him, Wood coaxes them into action and reaction, developing the relationships, searching for the significant movement to the subtly simple music. He loves to winkle out the nuance which betrays character or usurps etiquette. ('I'm intrigued by all forms of deceit; I feel secure with it.') And gradually there arises from them all – principals, conductor, producer – a mushroom-cloud of euphoria at resolving these beautiful and apparently artless phrases into something like a truth.

Ranged behind their tables along the breadth of the studio, the assistant producer, two repetiteurs, the senior stage manager Stella Chitty and her deputies are noting cues and marking scores, while at Davis's elbow the language coach Ubaldo Gardini urges the singers to ever greater subtleties of tempi, covering the written music with a hurricane of symbols on their interpretations. His *Don Giovanni* score, like many of his others, already preserves the idiosyncrasies of twenty casts and conductors over as many years – perhaps all that is left of their performances beyond human memory.

Behind him the assistant producer, who may supervise the opera's revival, pencils in his music with diagrams and descriptions of the singers' actions, even motives. An assistant stage manager is writing down entrance and exit cues and preparing requests to the technical department: 'Don Giovanni now needs a dagger in Act II Scene 3, to pick his teeth with: approx 8″ long from tip to base of handle – thin blade . . . Mr Wood would like blood to be visible on the spikes after the body has been removed. Donna Anna runs her hands over them . . . Don Giovanni and Leporello may need microphones in Act II Scene 3 to create an echo in the chapel. . . .'

Eventually the singers' pleasure spills into buffoonery. As Raimondi sings beneath her balcony – an improvised ladder – Te Kanawa reaches down and pulls his hair. Janowitz and Burrows take off their grotesque little face-masks and experiment with wearing them in other places, until the stage manager hides them away.

They near the opera's end. But the final scenes are unresolvable in studio rehearsal. They need the curved stairway, down which the avenging statue of the Commendatore, invited to dinner, will harrow the Don to his end. So they rehearse instead the hypnotic slow-march of the servants entering with the dinner platters, their decline into stealth and terror – an instability which moans in the music – and the laying of a place for the ghostly guest who may never come.

Wood explains where the stairway will fall, and tries to invoke it on the floor in an array of chairs and stage-flats. But the Don, Ruggero Raimondi, and the Commendatore, Gwynne Howell, have to confront each other on the level. Howell sings his entry in a sepulchral *sotto voce*, saving his voice. Then, at a moment of strange, throbbing strings which a piano can scarcely evoke, he pretends to descend the non-existent steps. Raimondi stares up. But they can neither envisage, nor time, their moves. They stop in frustration.

'How am I going to Hell?' Raimondi asks. He suggests pitching down from the stairway above the Commendatore.

'Magic,' says Wood.

But they have to wait for the stage rehearsal.

The opera producer must be deeply musical and patient. Few casts are uniformly willing to rethink familiar roles, and certain types of singer find these movement sessions meaningless. Acting detracts from their sense of self. 'If you could calculate egos,' says Te Kanawa, 'we singers would weigh tons.'

With this variable material the producer must dare to play. Peter Wood purposely clears his head of preconceptions before entering the studio – 'I believe that considered work is the most dangerous' – and trusts instead to the moment's gift, to the chemistry between the singers, the opera and himself. So too does John Copley, Covent Garden's principal producer. He approaches rehearsals sensing the effect he wants to make, but not yet knowing how he will make it. He starts with an acute sensitivity to vocal groupings and to the placing of pivotal scenery. In Act II of *Le nozze di Figaro*, for instance, 'You begin by asking yourself where the screen must be, and where the *gabinetto*, because these are the places where people will be for long stretches of vocal time.' Such fixtures – a screen, a door – become catalysts of invention. Copley loves Mozartian ingenuity, loves to develop the business within the work – critics sometimes accuse him of fussiness – and to indulge an old delight in composing stage pictures (he was once a designer) which will ravish the eye as well as pique the mind.

To all this the talents of Elijah Moshinsky, Covent Garden's chief guest producer, lend a sombre intellectual counterweight. It is the discovery of moral structure which energises him, and which makes a work meaningful. His production of Verdi's *Macbeth* inhabits a world of cosmic evil; it is ritualised tragedy, enacted in strong, brutal colours: blood, blackness. Its chorus of 140 was the largest ever heard on the Covent Garden stage. In the rehearsal studio, massed over a steep semicircle of creaking wooden steps – a mock-up of the stage set – they present a thunderous barricade of bodies and noise. Such numbers, if they are to escape the stasis of oratorio, have constantly to be moved about and broken up.

So Moshinsky fragments the inarticulate wall of their foursquare shoulders into stances, groups, ceremonies. Sometimes he stands far back from them as they sing, one hand bunched uncertainly at his mouth, trying to assess their shape, their movements. Behind him a repetiteur accompanies the pianist with airy beats of a chewed pencil, and the chorus master, John McCarthy, conducts with his hands. Moshinsky demands coldness, tension, economy of movement, tries to create men and women whom Macbeth's rule of terror has frozen into a collective desolation. He gives them motive, concentrates their thoughts. The same concepts return again and again. 'I don't want gesture . . . it must be cold, cold . . . this is the reign of the SS . . . keep your fists locked to your sides . . . a single uncommitted man will kill the show . . . it's got to be creepy . . . cold as steel . . . it's no good thinking about tea or football.'

The chorus is not so sure. Gusts of irreverence blow among them. Before a crucial male ensemble, the tenor section exhales a mutinous mutter about football, which rises where they are crowded together behind the set, awaiting their entrance. Moshinsky asks for silence. The piano strikes up, and the first group shambles on.

He flushes with anger. 'I'm not interested in this!' Now there is silence. He sends them back.

They start again. And the coldness is there. An indeterminate mass in their jeans and nondescript polo-necks and jackets, they thicken like robots over the stage. They act above all through the music. They grow animated when it sounds. Sometimes individual singers, during moments of action when the piano is silent, chant the phrases softly to themselves, as if they could not feel without them.

With the arrival of the conductor, Riccardo Muti, it ceases to be apparent where the territories of producer and conductor begin and end. Muti hears dramatic directives in Verdi's music: entrances, ways of walking, pauses. A conductor could usurp the producer's role by deducing everthing from it.

In the clinical studio, under the fluorescent lighting, he, Moshinsky and his Lady Macbeth, Renata Scotto, attempt the sleepwalking scene which precedes her death. She has never sung the role before. But the music trembles in a pulsing, dreamlike river, and tells her how to walk.

Moshinsky is unhappy. 'It's too beautiful,' he says. 'It's too balletic.' He wants her sleepwalk tense: the nightmare of a regressive child.

She returns thoughtfully up the steps. Her face is rounded, deceptively child-like. She looks unsuited to the part. Now Moshinsky directs her entry fast, agitated, before the gliding music plays at all. He sees movement patterns in his characters, and hers should be hard and serpentine. But she says: 'It was wrong. I didn't feel anything. I have to find the musical moment in which to move.'

Moshinsky wants neurosis, pain. But there is no pain in the music. So he surrenders his interpretation, and when Scotto tries again she glides down *lentamente* (as the score says) to the rippling notes, her face and extended hand suddenly eloquent.

She completes her long aria at the forefront of the stage. It is a reverie of remembrance, jolted by self-horror. In her mind there reverberates the midnight tolling bell of Duncan's murder. But it is only in her mind. Producer and conductor stand close to her as she sings. The piano thunders behind them. Muti's eagle nose and eyes project an almost violent sensitivity. His hands conduct so close that they are nearly kneading her face, while Moshinsky stands behind her, trying to feel alongside her and to deduce how she must act. Torn between these two demands – the educated eye and the educated ear – she sings in her dream to Macbeth, whom she must imagine by her side, her eyes grown wide, like pale buttons. The doll-like charm has gone. As she half wakens from her sleepwalk and realises she is alone, the territory of conductor and producer elide again, and it is Moshinsky who is nurturing in her a vocal colour to match her bewilderment, while her body droops and her aria dies back into infantile dreaming. This time conductor and producer agree. The moment is there in the music, in the words, in the singer's muted and heartbroken voice.

When Muti rehearses the chorus alone, he elicits in singing the same tension as Moshinsky had demanded in acting (they had agreed on a mutual approach months before.)

'*Staccatissimo!* It must be *nastier. Molto staccato! Trk-trk-trk. . . .*'

With finesse but no strength of voice, he sings them the shape and colour of the phrases, adding bite, coldness, all the time.

They radiate around him on chairs six deep, dotting their scores with symbols as he speaks. Heavy and comfortable, they look like a random cross-section of the British populace. Few of the 75-strong resident company have suffered the intense training of the Ballet or orchestra. Some have come late to their profession; they have been schoolteachers, nurses, town planners, naval ratings, lured away by the gift of a voice. Most of them have longed, at some time, to be soloists – the chorus is sprinkled with voices of great individual beauty – but the chances of success, in so competitive a profession, are slender. At Covent Garden they audition for the lesser roles; but if they want to rise higher, they must cut loose and advance alone. Among the men, especially, there is some disappointment. Unlike many of the fiercely motivated and disciplined dancers, they have probably opted for a low-paid security. The pride of belonging to one of the finest opera choruses in the world dwindles as they stand for long Wagnerian hours in stifling tabards, surcoats, undercoats, fur-trimmed hats, helmets, trying to recall the wellspring of their singing, their actions. Half their concentration is devoted simply to standing still or not fainting, and they long to be diversified, as in *Peter Grimes* or *Les Contes d'Hoffmann*, instead of merged into a liveried mass.

There is fear, too, that a chorus endangers the voice. You can float along on your neighbour's technique, they say, and never truly hear your own sound. But every three years they are subject to nerve-ridden auditions. Some conceive the voice almost as independent of them, like a tyrannical child. They grow afraid for it, sacrifice to it, listen to its changes as a dancer listens to his body. But unlike the dancer, they cannot compensate for weakness in one organ by relying on another. The dancer is ruled by a parliament of muscles and limbs, but the singer suffers under a single despot. Sopranos hear its range descend as their abdominal muscles slacken in the menstrual period (and sometimes delay this with the pill). And the strongest voice can quickly lose its beauty through natural causes, and there is no stopping it.

With all this, the chorus members bring an extrovert ebullience to their work, as if their personalities, like their voices, were lodged in the front of the face. Many are Welshmen and Scots. Fanned around Muti in a dense semicircle, the women look attentive and dedicated, while the men exude a robust British individualism. The bass section resembles a rugger scrum; the tenors – traditionally the hardest ranks to fill (the true tenor voice is rare) – are full of Welsh humour and anarchy.

They must all be acutely adaptable. Just as the Ballet can tune itself uniquely to contrasting dance modes, performing Balanchine and Ashton one night, Petipa or Bournonville another, so the chorus – perhaps because of the neutral, rather white timbre of the British voice – can embrace foreign styles and languages with uncanny fluency. Probably nowhere but in their native countries are the rich Italian vowels and double consonants, or the guttural, philosophical German sound or the coloured profundities of Russian more naturally sung.

*Opposite: violinist gazing at the stage in an interlude between playing; behind him, conductor Edward Downes*

It is the chorus master, John McCarthy, who has prepared the singers before the conductor's arrival, and who has tried to anticipate him. A choral veteran, he assumed directorship of the Covent Garden ensemble in 1980. He was Sir Thomas Beecham's chorus master for five years, and has trained choruses for over ninety operas with almost every leading maestro in the world. From this experience, he senses what will be demanded in tempi, colour, phrasing, and prepares it.

The demands which Muti makes of the chorus are reiterated to the orchestra in rehearsal. Within minutes he has imposed himself by a seismic inner energy. For a while he perches on the high conductor's stool, but the first *fortissimo* wrenches him up. His formal jacket is thrown away; a working pullover appears underneath. 'Strings *nastier*, please. Not *che-che-che*, but *rat-tat-rat-tat. Nasty.*' His own voice becomes hard and incendiary. Already he has created a terrible tension. The brass crashes out – he is happy here – the woodwinds skirl back. '*Moltissimo crescendo!*' He acts it out for them, vehement but economical, no flourish, unbreakably controlled. 'Sustain the last note. . . . Now, a shock! Crash! Strings! Give me *drr-drr-drr.*' Then, suddenly, he is appealing for a more emotional legato from the violins. 'No. Longer, longer, longer. . . .' His outsplayed fingers tremble, and he elicits a completely different string sound now, sustained, shimmering, effervescent, gliding away into nothing.

From the conductor's rostrum the acoustic is cruel, dead and transparent. He can hear every fault. The sounds rise about him unbalanced. Solti used to spend part of his first orchestral rehearsals sitting far back in the auditorium, merely to calculate the musical balance. But the same dry acoustic carries the stage sound clearly, its enunciation crisp, even to the softest choral *pianissimi*. The pit's shape thins and elongates the orchestra and aggravates the conductor's old problem of synchronising the brass on his far right with the horns on his far left. Some conductors counteract its length and darkness by the 'Grecian urn technique' – deep, scooping motions of the hands, more visible than the one-dimensional stroke of the baton.

The players say they can assess a conductor's quality within fifteen minutes (they have ugly tricks to test his expertise). They are merciless on the incompetent, and they do not admire the easy-going. But recently a galaxy of international maestros has refined and enriched their performance. In less than three years, between 1979 and 1981 alone, they played under Mehta, Haitink, Maazel, Muti, Böhm, Carlos Kleiber and Solti. They quickly sense the rhetoric of different batons, arms, voices. Every conductor has a different language. Giulini's is an athletic cataclysm, whereas Klemperer – fragile, seated, almost immobile – conveyed everything he needed for his *Fidelio* by the frailest pulse of the hand. Where Muti might demand *trk-trk-trk*, Haitink will say: 'I want the dotted notes accurately spaced.' Böhm, and sometimes Kleiber, were performed far behind the beat. And during Solti's directorship, he and the orchestra would laugh over the esoteric semaphore (you had to watch his elbows) which had developed between them.

After the turn of the century, when the curved pit was enlarged and squared, its form no longer reflected the bas-relief baffle above the proscenium, and the noise from its corners ascended, as it still does, unechoed to the ceiling. Worse still, the rail between players and auditorium closes off the sound of those seated against it. In the long, dry ravine of the pit, they must assemble in quixotic formation to achieve a blended tone. Usually the first violins are massed around the conductor's feet, the second relegated to the rail. The woodwind, central in a symphony orchestra, are pressed to his left, with the horns behind them. The acoustic carries no resonance, no bloom. The brass and wood-

The mezzanine under the stage is the storage depot for large musical instruments, and the scene of impromptu practising, top. Right: a double bass player from the stage band of *Don Giovanni* descending to the mezzanine. Above: percussion player beneath the lip of the stage

wind compensate by brighter overtones, the strings by greater roundness and *vibrato*. So the pit shapes them both musically and physically.

The space beneath the stage canopy is hated: in that resounding well, a person hears only himself. On evenings when the percussive drums and cymbals are vital, this valley of aural death is occupied by the double basses. But on other nights it houses the percussion section, who languish here with their view of the conductor obstructed by the backs of the double-bass players – but a more harmonious sound arises from the orchestra.

Like soldiers on a battlefield, the players know only what is happening immediately around them. The harmonies they receive are distorted. The brass rarely hears the wind (who may be persecuted by the horns behind them). The trumpets, receiving no echo from themselves, must listen to the strings for their tempi. The rear seat of violinists is nagged by the percussion; and the hindmost 'cellos, seated in the blasting-path of the trumpets, can be drowned out even to themselves (a 'cellist on a *Swan Lake* night might as well be deaf).

Something of this is familiar to symphony orchestras, but not all. Sunk beneath the level of the auditorium, the Opera House players have an illusion of invisibility. The audience which kindles a concert platform is not there. Often the pit is grossly crowded – more than a hundred players cram together for the *Ring* cycle or Strauss's *Elektra*, and even spill into the adjoining stalls circle – but few even glimpse the stage. They play for disembodied voices and thumping feet, sometimes underpinning artists whose musical habits they despise (long-note tenors, international ballerinas). More intently than a symphonist, they must watch the conductor as he follows stage action which may at any moment falter. No symphony orchestra has to muster the stamina and concentration

*Zubin Mehta and Jon Vickers in a rehearsal break of* Tristan und Isolde

required for the *Ring* cycle, or to play a piece which has gone unperformed since five nights before.

The orchestra at its worst feels jaded, unnoticed. Its 121 members – the largest body of orchestral players in Britain – escape both the stimulus and the itinerancy of those symphony orchestras which may attract the most gifted young players. Their curriculum (fourteen rehearsals or performances a fortnight, plus overtime) is spattered with their own outside engagements, but the Opera House remains security, home.

Their peculiar excellence – their playing is as consistently fine as that of any true opera orchestra in the world – is due in part to organisation. Whereas the players in other great houses will interchange from performance to performance, those at Covent Garden are assigned to individual operas and ballets. So a conductor knows that the same players whom he rehearses will perform with him: an obvious, but unique, blessing. No German house can match this; and at the Staatsoper the Vienna Philharmonic can lose sixty members to a concert on a single night. The Covent Garden orchestra's standing has never been higher. There was a time when the string section was weaker than the rest, but this is no longer so – it now plays with a clean brilliance. The influence of guest conductors, the respect of the players for Colin Davis, their participation in recordings under his baton (eighteen operas in his first ten years) – all these have spurred their enthusiasm and enhanced their musicality.

By the time the orchestra is being rehearsed in an opera, the wardrobe and production departments are far advanced in materialising it. The costume staff hope to effect two fittings on singers, three on dancers, and may anticipate these by prototype sessions using groups of four or five (or even a dress-stand) to assess the suitability of fabrics and the cutters' styling.

At a first true fitting, perhaps ten weeks before dress rehearsal, the designer and wardrobe staff gauge dresses still only roughly cut and tacked together. Many designers inspect the costumes of the full chorus or *corps de ballet*, amending each one. The questions to the artists are always the same. To singers: Can you hear? Can you breathe and move your jaws? To dancers: Can you keep it on? What movements do you do?

By the second fitting, two weeks before the dress rehearsal, all but the final garnish – lace, braid, appliqué, tassels, buttons – will be in place. But by then the whole stage setting is nearly complete, and the designer's model of nine months before has sprouted into a hundred artifices and complications. In the production workshops, fragrant with fir and pine, twelve men cut and shape rostra and screens in a whirring of ripsaws and fretsaws, band-saws and circular saws, producing scenery which must last for fully twenty years. Even the thread-like shafts of the 24-foot-high side-flats, tapering upwards from a $1\frac{1}{2}$-inch base, are each cut whole from the core of a pine. When the stage is artificially raked, the ramp built out beyond the safety curtain must be sawn from hard wood, while the colossal weight of the iron curtain itself descends on a seam of West African mahogany.

At these workshops the scenic cloths are outstretched flat in the American and Continental way, so they may be overlaid by gnarled textures of paint or elaborated with areas of gauze. The design of other cloths is allocated to the opera house studio itself, whose artists work by the 'English method', standing up. It is a gaunt, skylit chancel of a place, where two giant vertical frames, dimmed by paint and dirt, travel up and down on weighted ropes from the stage below. Shelves and trolleys burgeon with seductively-labelled paint pots – Vandyke crystals, titanium, Dutch pink – and kettles grumble on charred gas-rings, boiling the water to break down aniline dyes. The studio artists paint on canvas or calico cloths often sixty-five feet long. They seal the fabric with a clear primer, outline the design in charcoal and begin to paint in broad, thin washes, which will leave the canvas supple and the picture unsplintered when rolled up. Helped by two mobile air compressors which produce steady paint textures – a fine mist at high pressure, a dotted patina at low – a pair of artists can complete a sixty-five-foot canvas within two weeks.

Back in the production workshops, twelve other craftsmen with multifold and unexpected talents concoct the stage properties. Gem-encrusted reliquaries and chasubles for *Lohengrin*, a corruscating fish for auction in *The Rake's Progress*, the translucent skeletons (plastic and polythene tubing) which trickle like dehydrated spiders from the barbed wire of *Thérèse* – these are as nothing compared to the mechanical harp for *Les Contes d'Hoffmann* (equipped with three tiny inner motors), which entered the stage alone while its key-topped stem turned eerily round and round, and a pair of bodiless hands plucked its strings with a ghostly caress.

The craftsmen's most handy materials are malleable and synthetic: polystyrene, rubber and glass fibre, paper rope. They work in disposable boiler suits among glass and chemical fumes, at lathes, in spraying-booths. Above all they produce furniture – from silk-upholstered 'Regency' to the rustic benches for *Coppélia* – and a variegated host of statues. One man may take a week and a half to sculpt a life-size statue in polystyrene, and although the 24-strong conclave of prayerful saints and apostles for *Don Giovanni* burst into life in less than a month, these figures were not what they seemed. They were built from chopped-up and reassembled shop dummies. Their added musculature was of carved synthetic foam, and their vestments composed of cloth dipped in foul-smelling animal dyes, draped around them and dried solid. Their hair was of insulating rope picked out by streaks of glue, and their pious figures were covered at last with a skin of butter muslin and textured to pass for marble.

Macbeth *in rehearsal. Part of the 140-strong chorus assembling on a mock-up of the stage set*

**Macbeth**. Conductor Riccardo Muti rehearses his soloists. Left: Renata Scotto sings Lady Macbeth; below: Muti at the piano with (left to right) Renata Scotto, Robert Lloyd (Banquo) and Renato Bruson (Macbeth); and with producer Elijah Moshinsky. Opposite above: view of the orchestra stalls and assembled chorus from the summit of the *Macbeth* set; below: in orchestral rehearsal

**Macbeth**. Opposite above: Riccardo Muti in a rehearsal break with Elijah Moshinsky (seated right) stage manager Stella Chitty (centre) and John Tooley, standing. Below: witches in rehearsal

Left: in the paint frame above the stage, where a half-finished backcloth for *The Sleeping Beauty* hangs, a repetiteur with earphones and television conducts an offstage band in Act I. Below: children's coach Jean Povey prepares one of her girls for the Apparition Scene, in which Renato Bruson as Macbeth is terrorised by the phantom kings

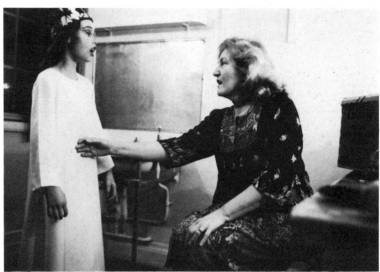

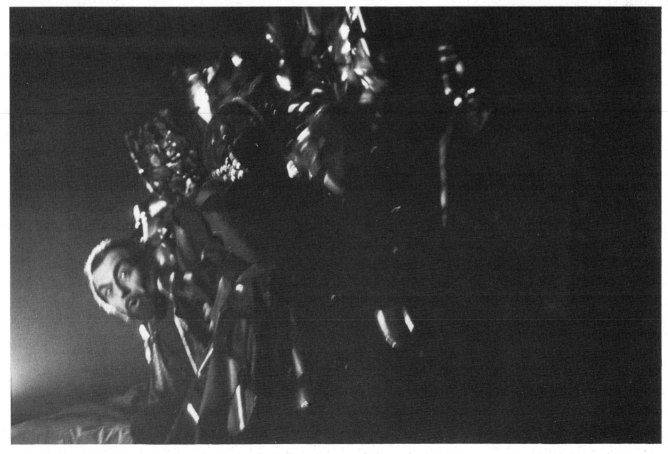

**Macbeth**. Riccardo Muti conducting

Opposite: Renato Bruson as Macbeth

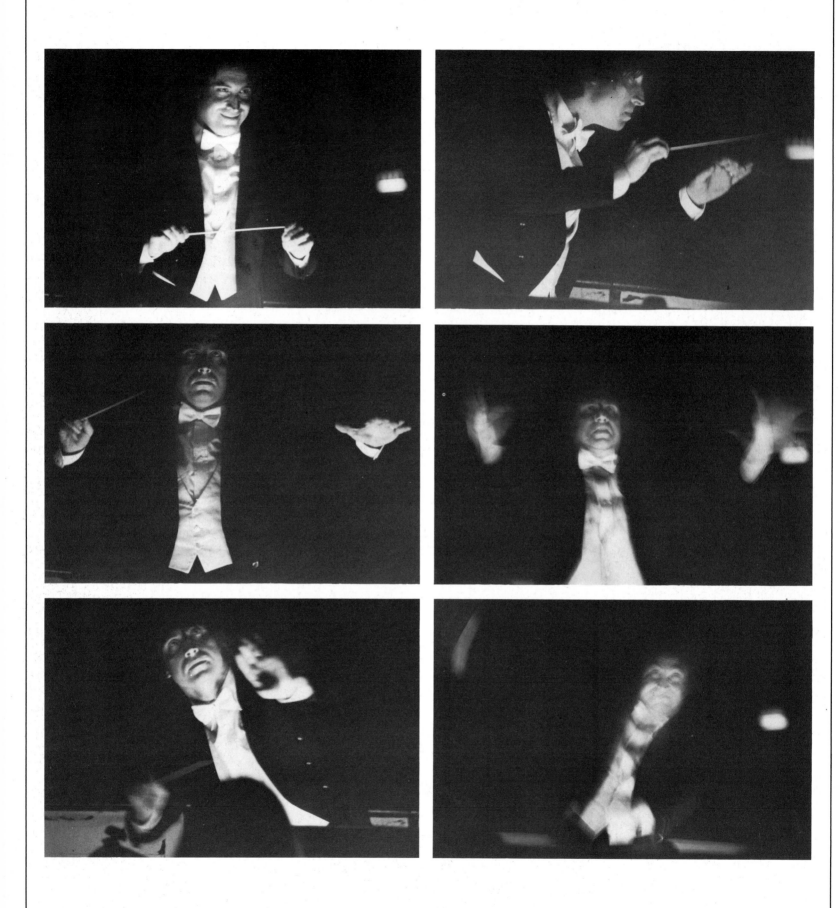

**Macbeth**. Opposite: the last act. Elijah Moshinsky, above,
in dress rehearsal, directs the chorus of refugees; below:
the curtain falls

**Gloria**. The cast gathers round Kenneth MacMillan for
instructions after stage rehearsal. Overleaf: moments from
*Gloria*, with Stephen Beagley (sewing slipper); Julian
Hosking partnering Jennifer Penney; Linda Moran
supported by Anthony Molyneux

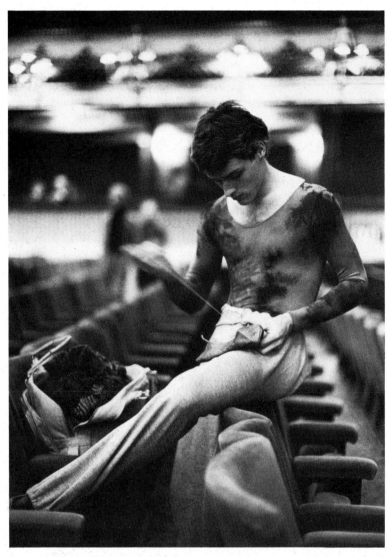

**Gloria**. Opposite: the closing scene. From the audience viewpoint, above, the cast appears to depart downhill, but in fact descends into the lowered stage elevator

Stage hands rush away the flats of *Gloria* moments after the curtain falls, while Wayne Eagling is still making for the dressing-rooms

**Don Giovanni**. A 60-foot wide backcloth being created in the paint frame on a base of white primer, its design first sketched in with a long-handled charcoal stick

**Don Giovanni**. In the production workshops prop-makers transform dismembered shop dummies into religious statuary, using as models the drawings of designer William Dudley, top right, or even their own bodies. Bottom right: carpenter's bench

Opposite: stage hands fix the runners of the *Don Giovanni* colonnades, and assemble its upper platform; designer William Dudley, below right, pleads with production manager Jeffrey Phillips to make it work

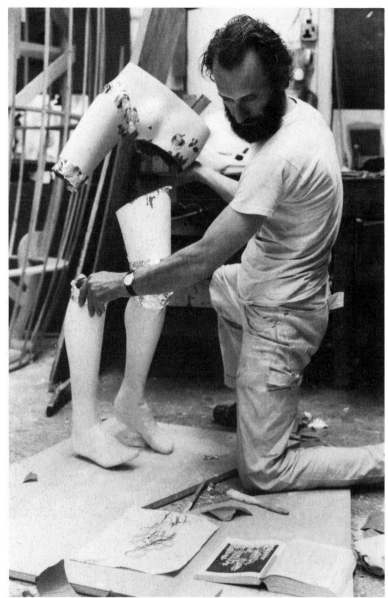

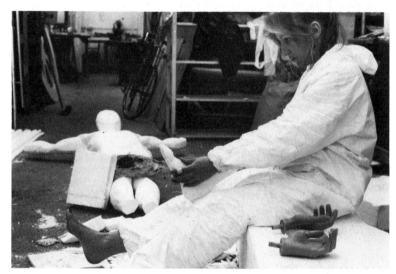

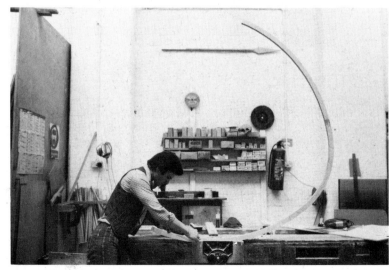

**Don Giovanni** in rehearsal. Post-mortem: Colin Davis
with producer Peter Wood, kneeling, Helga Schmidt and
Davis' personal assistant Betty Scholar, left

Opposite: lighting session on the colonnades, and
easing the porticoes

**Don Giovanni** in performance. Opposite above: Italian language coach Ubaldo Gardini (second from right) prompts from a concealed seat behind the proscenium. Below: chorus and opera ballet dancers mingle in the rustic wedding scene.

Below: Ruggero Raimondi, Kiri te Kanawa and John Tomlinson (left) during a break in rehearsal. Before the first night a dressmaker, right, gingerly carries Donna Elvira's Act I costume to Kiri te Kanawa's dressing-room. Raimondi jokes with Ubaldo Gardini in an interval, and leaves the stage after curtain-calls

**Don Giovanni** in performance. Opposite: Kiri te Kanawa
as Donna Elvira, Ruggero Raimondi as Giovanni

Dismantled sets being carried down Floral Street

Crush Bar party after the first night of *Don Giovanni* – preparations. Bottom left: Sir Francis Sandilands, chairman of the production's sponsor, Commercial Union Assurance, speaks to the guests. Bottom right: front-of-house staff clearing away afterwards

Opposite: half an hour before curtain-up the head linkman reports to the house management the numbers of front-of-house staff present, and the barmen juggle with bottles

Opposite: in the flies

At the former stage door: Kiri te Kanawa and Sir Colin Davis sign autographs, while assistant general director Paul Findlay and Sir John Tooley are in discussion inside

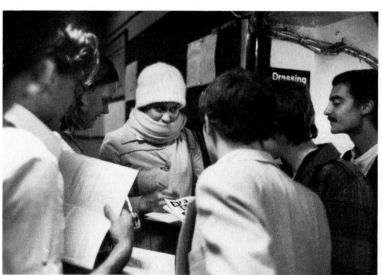

# ON STAGE

No studio can vie with the stage. It is the final, cruel arbiter. From dawn, through all the day and half the night, it is the focus of performing casts, electricians or stage hands, and even on Sundays it is given over to twelve-hour technical sessions for assembling and lighting sets.

These Sunday marathons see the debut of each new production. The scenery is interlocked in a massive jig-saw which may take all day to complete. Far back in the darkened orchestra stalls, the producer, designer and lighting designer sit at a long desk and watch the lights wash and dim over the stage-picture half assembled there. The lighting designer, poring over a ground-plan and focusing-chart roughed out in rehearsals, builds up the scenes' light layer by layer out of darkness, laying it in ever-brightening strokes, until it achieves the right intensity or quietness. Two electricians sit beside him with a monitor and relay his orders to the switchboard at the back of the grand tier. On the set the stage management go through the movements of the absent artists, their speech small and discoloured in the theatre's immensity.

The stage becomes the arena of haunting possibilities. Light alters the emotion of a set, as music does. It isolates, warms, mystifies, freezes, like a visual tone-poem. At Covent Garden the lighting designer commands almost a thousand lamps and a prismatic luxuriance of colour filters. Its circuits have been constantly updated. They suffuse the scenery with a level flood out of the amphitheatre, radiate a calm backlight from a grid set eighty feet deep in the stage's recesses, or break over the boards from lamps ranged above the balcony boxes and from perches and bridges around the proscenium arch. A constellation of other lamps dangles above the stage on bars of soft-lighting battens, or is clustered in banks of powerful, low-voltage bulbs, a hundred or more together, which drown the set beneath in a hard, factual blaze. High up, in the gilded frieze around the dome, a concealed panel glides back from follow-spots which shed their beams 150 feet to the stage, and which are manoeuvred with lordly accuracy, their intensity altered by a single guiding hand. In the amphitheatre, and on eight lamps nestled within the hub of the dome, automatic colour-change units can disgorge a carnival of atmospherics, while within the proscenium, on either side, a great square projector furnished with revolving discs sends snowstorms or thunderclouds raging across the set.

For all this bewildering galaxy, the cues are relayed softly by microphone from the stage manager's control panel; but only the spotlights from the dome and fly galleries are manually operated; the rest are effected in their preordained order by a computer installed in 1977.

Despite this richness, the lighting designer remains unbemused by the multiplicity of permutations, but is seeking to realise a picture already in his mind. For ballet, as for opera, he is illuming near-empty sets. So precious is stage-time, that to light the actual dancers in rehearsal, as a foreign or a smaller company would, is impossible. Only a few actors or ballet students stand about on stage in place of a massed *corps* or a headlong *pas de deux*, and from this he must transfigure the light into a living character, intrinsic to the dancers, sensitised and changing in ways superfluous to opera.

The Ballet's lighting designer, John B. Read, works from detailed diagrams of the dancers' movements, sketched out during studio rehearsals, with colour notes on their costumes. Faced by the set, he develops ideas which he has already conceived, and draws his light's emotion from the dance pattern itself. 'I never say during rehearsals "What sort of effect shall I make?" I say "What am I getting from the dancers?" With ballet lighting you have to be with the dancers all the way. It's a very instinctive thing.' This austere search for essence is resistant to any but the most purposeful toying with lamps. Even the phantasmagoric billows of Loie Fuller's *Isadora* drapery were drenched or undermined with light until they had achieved the right quality of Art Nouveau preciosity. They became hideous and glacial under spotlight, were frozen and flattened to nothing, then resurrected piecemeal until their brilliant turquoise and gold shone with a sickly loveliness, dribbling violet at the rims like some oleaginous sea-creature – a fairytale jellyfish or ray.

Read, meanwhile, sits at the production desk beside Kay and MacMillan, who is mentally peopling the blank stage with his dancers, and directs the electricians in the arithmetical jargon of their 240 lighting circuits: 'Can we add in 140 to point five? . . . Show me 59 point six . . . kill 29 and bring 78 full and 81 full and 86 to 7 and 23 to full. . . .' – and the stage blushes into light.

But these sessions also show the first, ominous lapses in production: doors which won't open, cinematic projections which dissipate and fail, wheeled scenery whose tracks buckle, jam or squeal like pigs. The production manager Jeffrey Phillips is on hand even on a Sunday to register troubles, and the ballet stage manager Keith Gray busy co-ordinating the movement of props and transition of scenes.

As rehearsals reach the stage, perhaps two weeks before the opening night, production dilemmas proliferate and intertwine with musical ones, time presses harder, personal tensions rise. In opera these two vital weeks on stage sometimes see a shuffling of power-structures among visiting conductors, producers, star singers, which may not reach a first night peacefully. The early, piano rehearsals are the province of the producer; the later, orchestral sessions the prerogative of the conductor; but each attends all of them, and may invade the territory of the other brusquely or surreptitiously, while the singers try (or don't) to split their energies between the two.

Standing on the pit rostrum alone, and circled by arcs of empty orchestra chairs, the maestro conducts a solitary pianist as the first rehearsals go falteringly forward. In the prompter's box, hidden by an enclosure under the lip of the stage, another repetiteur guides the singers according to their need, sometimes accompanying them almost word for word in the Italian way, more often pointing the vocal entrances and calling out cue words as the Germans do. Occasionally during a finished performance, if the orchestra is playing softly or a singer standing far back, this phantom counterpoint can be heard in the audience.

All through the piano rehearsals, at worst, the singers feel the music dulling in them. The studio's intimacy is replaced by a cold travesty of the set in which they will perform.

*Opposite. Rear wall of the stage: backcloths stacked beneath shrouded lamps and light battens*

Scene-changes become long campaigns, in which cliff-like chunks of scenery are pushed miserably back and forth by sweating stage hands. A hundred technical faults swim to light. Props aren't there or don't work – are too heavy, fragile, long, short. Wheels stick. Spears break. Curtain-rings whine. Front-cloths and gauzes hitch against one another as they descend, or strike the scenery and even the singers, unaligned.

And now the singers have to redefine their movements. The makeshift sets in the studio, if any, never accurately reproduce those on stage, and suddenly the ascent and descent of stairs, the crossing of a platform or a terrace, may happen in a different time. In these big spaces, the small gesture is lost. It must be projected again, stronger. So must the voice – no longer cosseted by the studio's sonority, but probing the drier acoustic of the house.

The producer sits at the production desk, microphone in hand, and watches how the patterns which he has created radiate or weaken. Sometimes he mounts to the stage by a steel gangplank laid across the orchestra pit, spreads or redistributes the singers or redefines their movements. The scenery excites him to new ideas, aborts old ones. His assistant, who has been effecting his orders on stage, dogs his steps and notes down action-changes in the score. But for the conductor, the emotional temperature has plummeted. His singers, distracted by acting demands, preserve their voices by marking the arias *sotto voce*, like ghosts whispering together. After the closeness of the studio, his figure in the pit looks far away to them. He waits to rekindle the music in orchestral rehearsals.

Even *Don Giovanni*, after its studio euphoria, musically leaks away. Its huge, green-veined palace, studded with declamatory statues, jolts in its tracks and tyrannises the whole production. The singers feel far upstage, their intimacy with the audience un-

*Changing lights*

achieved. Scene by scene the producer Peter Wood tries to recover it. Once he shouts in exasperation: 'Working here is like pushing treacle upstairs!' Elaborate moments, such as the plunge of the Don into Hell, have to be resolved out of a myriad possibilities. Wood sets Raimondi slithering along the bannisters of the coiling staircase until he is twisted into Hades below; then Raimondi tries casting himself from the stairs on to a concealed lift which lowers him away; and finally he grapples with Howell's Commendatore perilously high above the stair-well and crashes down the steps in a long, tumbling fall into the inferno.

After the piano rehearsals' struggle for dramatic interpretation, an interim musical session (a '*Sitzprobe*') forms a reassuring bridge into the costly and time-dogged orchestral rehearsals. Seated on hard little chairs along the stage, the principals sing the opera through with the orchestra, and forget the beat of the studio piano in this lovelier but more elusive plenitude.

As they launch on true orchestral rehearsals, unity at first evades them. The orchestra is still feeling for the singers' voices, and they for its. Faced by the blacked-out auditorium, the singer is aware of noises in the wings, in the stalls, along the overhead bridges where the lamps dangle and glow at him like dim, warm eyes. The conductor speaks to him from the pit through a microphone, appeals for nuances of sound which he has lost. 'You split yourself into so many parts,' says Janet Baker. 'On the concert platform the sense of unity is far clearer; on the opera stage, even in late rehearsals, your attention is caught by a hundred other factors, and all the things that could go wrong.' Close behind the conductor, a repetiteur notes down his strictures like a private secretary – mistimings, poor diction, orchestral imbalances.

*Removing props*

At this juncture the offstage bands, muffled from the auditorium by an intervening scenic cloth or relayed by loudspeaker from a distant room, become nagging pitfalls. In the echoing heights of the paint studio, or far backstage, a repetiteur, listening to the orchestra through headphones and watching the conductor's beat on a closed-circuit television, synchronises his knot of singers or players as best he can. When both orchestra and band play rapid, rhythmic music, as in *Don Carlos* or *Un ballo in maschera*, this double-act teeters above an abyss, and for much of *Lohengrin* the wings and paint studio are dense with clusters of chorus, trumpeters, drummers, trombone-players or a 22-strong band, which must all be minutely blended with the orchestra.

As the conductor seeks to integrate the sounds from stage and pit, calling up to the chorus above the quieter music, the producer's time is almost over, and he may fear that the thing is sliding out of his hands. The performers are thinking of the music now, of the orchestra, and he can intervene little. Sometimes he sees his ideas changed or forgotten, the singers' motivations lost. The conductor may demand that a section of the chorus be merged closer until they sound superb but look banal. Flamboyant gestures arise un-rehearsed among the stars. The visual patterns are broken. During pauses the producer dashes up among the singers to correct or reinvent; but usually he remains at the back of the auditorium, and talks by radio-microphone to his assistant producer, who prowls on stage surreptitiously in headphones, and repositions chorus or principals as they sing. Sometimes whole themes and actions are abandoned altogether and remain to haunt the stage in unreclaimed fragments – aborted movements, furniture brought in for one pur-pose but redeployed for another.

In *Macbeth* Muti several times froze the stage action altogether to attain maximum musical clarity, and Moshinsky could only break up the oratorio-like palisade of the chorus's 140 bodies by dribbling ribbons of light among them. For lighting often con-tinues to the end. Even in the last rehearsal, an experiment with overhead lamps suddenly dehumanised the chorus's black helmets and banners into an ant-like scuttle of soldiery, while the next moment they were backlit – the banners pellucid, barely martial at all, and the downstage troops transformed to shades.

Slowly, as the music gains momentum, the singers grow confident, their voices cushioned in orchestral velvet. Around them the warm but clear acoustic of the audi-torium answers them back. If it is not as resonant as Bayreuth or the Metropolitan, the Paris Opéra or the London Coliseum, it is more intimate, kinder to the lower voice ranges, and more sensitive to the enunciated word. Carpets and velvet chairs soak up the reverberation, but the horseshoe tier-fronts comfortably return the singer's voice, and although every operatic stage is dappled with blind or favourite spots (La Scala's are notorious), that at Covent Garden is happily almost consistent.

With each rehearsal, the stage props multiply in their docks in the wings. The offal for *Macbeth*'s witches goes to join the peacock fans for *L'Africaine*, the candlesticks for *Tosca* and the crooks of *Daphnis and Chloë*. And as the singers climb into their gowns or armour, a new dimension unfolds. Men who felt foolish flourishing spears while dressed in jeans and sweaters, now surprise themselves. The real self shelters behind the acting self, and is liberated into a licensed irresponsibility. The voice itself becomes more coloured, more characterful, more integrated.

*Macbeth*, even by this stage, was finely tuned. Chorus and orchestra say that they can count on the fingers of one hand the conductors who elicit a truly knit response from both stage and pit – and Muti is one. As the witches ooze and seep across a slate-mine of a set, he draws from them an infernal, sarcastic patter which chills the blood. Sometimes they flitter with uncanny lightness, as if they were less hags than an area of unease in Macbeth's mind. They are at once squalid and ethereal. Against the black steps, in their black clothes, the wholesome faces of the chorus, turned corpse-like in mauve and bluish veils, are lit faintly by shifting lights. Behind them the steps rise to a stone heath, spiked with winter trees which have never flowered, and behind this again the backcloth shows a raging sky as if a city were on fire far away: the flames of Sodom.

But Muti cries to the witches: 'Too nice! *Nastier, nastier!*'

When they vanish in front of Macbeth's eyes, they do so a second too late. They complain that they can't see their feet. Muti asks that they start to disappear earlier, so that the final musical pause is only short. But Moshinsky does not want to diffuse them. He goes backstage and has the wings lit so the witches can see their exodus. They start again. The music whispers and glows. This time, among the wild and manically chanting veils, the headphoned face of an assistant producer is bobbing back and forth, speeding the witches' exit. With every bar of the orchestra they dissolve like fungus over the steps, and as the music stops the stage falls bare and unhaunted.

During these earliest dress rehearsals, the singers are once again adjusting their timing as voluminous period dresses slow the ascent of a stairway or the advance to a balcony. Time is now a hounding presence. Four days before the opening night, a final piano rehearsal offers the producer his last chance to alter and polish. But sometimes, even at this stage, complete scenes have scarcely been blocked out, especially in the longer Wagner operas, and must be developed at a gallop. Next day a full-scale orchestral rehearsal

*Mirella Freni between Acts in a* La Bohème *rehearsal*

belongs to the conductor, who may exclude whole sections to alight on others which trouble him.

Two or three days before the premiere, the last, composite rehearsal, the 'General', brings muted optimism or panic. The stalls fill with administrative and music staff and press photographers. Backstage, members of the production wardrobe and the running wardrobe mingle in a last-minute turmoil. After the final curtain-calls, the auditorium becomes a whirlpool of assessments and corrections. Now the stage management is in the firing-line – the producer bemoaning a late entry or a vanished prop, the lighting designer complaining about a lost spotlight cue. Everybody is suddenly making notes. On stage Sir John Tooley, the conductor, the principals, the technical director and the production manager conjecture and confabulate together in pleased or haggling clusters. The producer is dictating changes for transmission to the singers, the designer worrying at the technical staff, while all around them the scenery is already being dismantled irretrievably, the sets for *Mayerling* gathering in the wings, or the newly-painted backdrop of *The Sleeping Beauty* descending behind.

A ballet itself suffers a hauntingly similar cycle. In its last studio rehearsals it may achieve a beauty and completeness. But both Ashton and MacMillan recoil from its transference to the stage. In that pitiless arena, they say, it seems at first to disappear. The dancers' moves fall into a new perspective. Like the singers, they must now redefine their steps more powerfully. Even the noise of their feet is less. They spin in a vacuum. Everything is momentarily paler, hollower, more disjointed.

A dancer's liberation from the judging studio staff of earlier rehearsals cannot compensate him for this isolation (and he knows they are still watching him). For months he has grown accustomed to the level light and mirror-clad security of the studio. Now, where once he danced with his mirror-image, however dimly perceived, there is suddenly only the vertiginous drop into the orchestra pit and the blackness of the auditorium beyond. His own body is objectively lost to him. He must seek a new balance. Some dancers unconsciously edge downstage towards the blackness; others retreat from it. *Pas de deux* become dislocated. The dancer's need to avoid dizziness by 'spotting' during pirouettes – twisting the gaze repeatedly on to a fixed point in front of him – is frustrated in the dark. A tiny blue spotting star, illumined at the back of the stalls circle, is said to have been installed at the request of Margot Fonteyn (but she cannot remember this).

Just as to the singer all stages are chequered by dead or resonant areas, so the Covent Garden boards are a dancer's minefield. The slats which seal the interstices between the big elevators create long, thin ridges and depressions, which can break a man's leg or overthrow a girl on pointe, and the unaligned edges of a trapdoor lie in wait near the prompt corner. Sometimes during a *pas de deux* one partner will murmur to another to avoid these corrugations by dancing farther up or downstage. But the boards are sanded or replaced as they become worn, and the laying of linoleum or of floorcloths merely conceals unevennesses, and brings troubles of its own. Linoleum is ugly and reflects the light; whereas a new cloth may wrinkle and move underfoot, and when old is often slippery or fragmented into a rough-and-smooth patchwork by rosin from the dancers' shoes.

Seated centre-stage during these first, desultory rehearsals, with his back to the empty auditorium, the choreographer concentrates on placing his dancers in their new space: deepening a *corps*, spreading a solo. Like singers saving themselves *sotto voce*, they do not dance full out, but mark their steps lightly, like musical thoughts. It is now that a hundred apparent simplicities of production – the eternal entrances and exits and linking of scenes – take on a malignant life and complication of their own. The set's props and raised areas create unanticipated opportunities and puzzles. And the burden of resolving them falls on the choreographer. It is as if in the straight theatre one man were both director and playwright.

Later in the rehearsal he retreats into the auditorium, and the dancers perform full out. Nothing is predictable. Massed *corps* scenes can quake into insignificance, a solitary *pas de deux* fill the stage. Spasmodically he dictates notes to the artistic administrator, Iris Law sitting beside him: points of theatre, faults in interpretation. And the stalls are now fretted with the critical gaze of others – choreologists and ballet masters, designer and wardrobe supervisor, technical and production staff, Norman Morrice, perhaps John Tooley; while the stalls circle thickens with silently watching dancers. The atmosphere is fitful, a little unhappy. At the end the dancers assemble on stage to receive a maelstrom of correction from the staff; and it is only a week before the ballet's first night.

Yet within two days the onslaught of fault-finding has dwindled, the stage blooms into fuller scenery and light, and the dancers climb into costume. Dress fills them with love-hate. Compared to their casual leotards, the best-made costume may constrict. Some of them – quick to impersonate in the studio – now stare into the mirror and must subtly rethink the characters they are dancing. Others adjust to fractionally slower movements, or to partnering a suddenly satin waist or a ballooning skirt.

The first dress rehearsal is a wardrobe mistress's nightmare. Things fall off, split, break, wrinkle up. But for the dancers there is an upsurge of exhilaration and humour. Costume, in spite of everything, enforces their presence. They start to move and feel differently. And to the choreographer – ideally – dress, scenery and light begin to merge with the dance in a sensory whole.

Merle Park, in the lamenting solos of *Isadora*, now advances downstage in a diaphanous white chiton. Momentarily she moves in remembered happiness, but the light is autumn, and the background dimmed to a Chinese whorl of turquoise and brown. The Grecian dress lends her an Ondine-like fragility. Her solo is the still heart of the ballet. Cradling her children's memory, she dances in a confluence of twilit light and green-blue back-drop, relinquishing her dead at last with long, desolate gestures into the void.

The first orchestral rehearsal brings the same enhancement and anxiety. The percussive themes familiar to the dancers through the studio piano are suddenly confused and interlaced by other harmonies. In the case of commissioned music, neither the cast nor the choreographer has ever heard the orchestration before (since musicians' fees prohibit recording for studio rehearsal). The piano rendering may insidiously have shortened long-held string passages and broadened more intricate moments – so with orchestra the dancers must adjust to the steps anew. Some modern scores, in particular – such as Schoenberg's and Webern's in *My Brother, My Sisters* – are scarcely reducible to piano transcription, and emerge unrecognisable in the first orchestral rehearsal a few days before the premiere. But like singers who feel exhilarated by the new orchestral luxuriance swelling under their voices, both choreographer and dancers, however taken by surprise, exult to hear their steps suffused in the sudden tremor of instruments.

But the orchestra sometimes plays less happily for ballet. Sunk in the pit, its musicians cannot see the drama they accompany. To those playing under the lip of the stage, the delicate-looking *pas de chats* of the *Swan Lake* cygnets passes overhead like a thunderstorm. Constant changes of the conductor's beat, especially in *Giselle* and the Tchaikovsky ballets, distort the music for reasons invisible to them, and final bars are habitually elongated so that dancers may end on time. Visiting stars often demand eccentric *tempi* and even in modern choreography the music may be bent to the steps. In the end, ballet conductors, sensitive to the capacities of different dancers, are faced by the choice of how much to inspire and extort from them, and how much to nurture and accompany.

The final rehearsals follow no smugly rising graph. Some even descend into shambles. Before the orchestra assembles in the pit at 10.30, the dancers have warmed up for little more than half their usual class-time, and emerge the more susceptible to injury. All the things which will soon become routine can founder into pandemonium. Last-minute changes to props or scenery may start a chain-reaction of confusion and suppressed panic. Backstage becomes a vortex of nervous dancers, bedevilled dressers, bemused stage hands. Troupes of extras – actors, children – congest the wings in bewildered throngs. Ballerinas running round the wings for lightning re-entries on stage miss their cues by gaping split-seconds. And as the rehearsal lumbers to its end, the dancers' morale is seen, after all, to be rather fragile, and their sense of corporate failure poignantly intense.

But by the 'general' rehearsal the fear is invisible again, and the fluster in scene-changes almost gone. At the production desk, set up in the stalls or grand tier, Read demands a last exactitude of light – the subtle aureole which beautifies a dancer's line; the designer scribbles down refinements of effect – taking in a belt, deepening a neckline – and the staff's notes have dwindled to a trickle. As the rehearsal ends, a sense of family involvement surges in the company. Soon the stage-floorcloth is being peeled away, and the electricians focusing other lights. But in the dressing-rooms, hours later, the wardrobe supervisor is still listing the changes relayed by designer and dressers, and is allocating garments to their costumiers for repair: 'Heighten Spanish hats . . . Hosking: paint braces brown . . . Drew: another cravat in crepe satin and a longer monocle string. . . .' She goes on working tiredly, carefully, while through the loudspeaker above the door the stage hands' shouts thin and vanish, and around her the dressers are laying out the wimples and gowns for the evening's *Lohengrin*.

Costumes, on the opening night, pass from the production wardrobe into the control of the running wardrobe, whose corridor-like rooms beetle high up in the house or are scattered as storage basements in old Mart and Southampton Streets. In a handful of domestic washing-machines and driers, which constantly break down through overwork, heavy operatic gowns and sweat-impregnated ballet clothes, often soiled with makeup, are drenched, tumbled and spun before every other performance. This and minor repairs consume the days of a permanent staff of thirty. The floor-trailing silk and lace operatic dresses, in particular, abrade and tear on the boards, and almost all are patched and stitched at the hems within a few months. The girls' ballet costumes fray around the waist from constant handling; and drooping tutus, whose twelve or thirteen gauze layers are intricately caught up with cotton, take a full working day to refurbish or brace with wire hoops.

Late cancellations are the wardrobe's special ordeal. Then they must telephone agents and opera houses for emergency measurements, quickly adapt the garments – an elaborate costume can be transformed within an hour – or confect a new outfit from the ward-

robe of other operas. Occasionally there is no time even for alterations. A last-minute substitute for *Norma* arrived as the opera started, suffered momentary hysterics as she heard the orchestra, but was already tearing off her clothes as she rushed backstage. Her dress did not meet at the back. The wardrobe mistress wrapped a cloak round her, increased her height by pushing cotton wool inside her headdress, and five minutes later she was singing on the stage, moving obediently to the signals of a production assistant in the wings.

The contrast between the multi-national Opera and the tight-knit Ballet creates different styles of stage management. Up and down the musical and theatrical echelons of the house, there are posts whose imprecision makes them as large or as insignificant as their occupants, and stage management is among these. In the absence of a producer for ballet, its stage manager Keith Gray intrudes his responsibility into the smooth running of all its props and changes. The dancers themselves are too disciplined to need control. The opera stage manager Stella Chitty, on the other hand, extends a mingled efficiency and tenderness to her singers, anticipates their worries, and sometimes needs her full staff

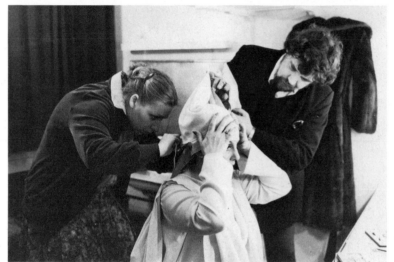

**Norma**. The mezzo-soprano Alexandrina Milcheva is rushed over from Vienna a few hours before curtain-up to take over the role of Adalgisa. Artistic administrator Helga Schmidt, top left, learns of her arrival at London airport while general manager Ande Anderson, a staff producer and repetiteur wait at the stage door. Milcheva arrives after the opera has started; Helga Schmidt encourages her in her dressing-room, above, the wardrobe mistress and wigmaster improvise her headgear, and Ande Anderson accompanies her to the stage. She only meets John Tooley and conductor Lamberto Gardelli, opposite, after Act I

of four to cue them on to the stage. She is the Opera's gentle dragon. When in rehearsal she demands (rhetorically) who is smoking illicitly in the orchestra pit, Sir Colin Davis guiltily removes his pipe.

The prompt corner (so-called) in the wings is the stage managers' cockpit. Standing at its control panel and leafing through a score, they relay cues and calls by microphone not only for lighting but to the artists' dressing-rooms and to every corner in the house. Through stagehands in the galleries they summon in the flying scenery; they operate the cue-lights in the wings and for the big elevators and concealed traps under the stage, and control the miniature red and green bulbs ('standby' and 'go') on the conductor's rostrum. From here, too, the house lights are dimmed in the auditorium, and the three-ton mohair velvet curtains raised and lowered by motors and counterweights at the touch of a lever. Beside the control panel a closed-circuit television shows both stage and orchestra (its tiny camera eye is beamed at the conductor just above the pit), and other televisions, hanging on both sides of the proscenium arch, relay a picture of the conductor – a figure glazed by lights, but perfectly visible – to singers who cannot see his baton from their position on stage. The more complex the placement of singers, the more precarious their musical accuracy becomes. The villagers who stare diagonally downstage to chant a pastoral greeting for the heroine of *Luisa Miller* are not gazing at her window at all, but watching the conductor's baton on a television. *Macbeth* needs four such televisions, *Lulu* six; and in *Lohengrin* the singers sometimes take their musical cues from the wings, where members of the music staff are levitated on ladders like Wimbledon umpires and conduct with torches to the beat of the maestro on televisions beside them.

The stage's facilities include theatrical effects operated by electricians and cued by the stage management. A powerful red lamp, shining through strips of cloth fanned and fluttering on a wire, projects the hearth-flames which flicker over the faithlessness of Manon and the death of Scarpia. Lightning flashes from boxes of magnesium-based powder, ignited by electricity. And at least three families of smoke invade the air. Smoke-boxes eject angry thunder-clouds such as curdle under the chariot of Carabosse in *The Sleeping Beauty* (a smoke which irritates singers' voices and can congeal to oil on stage and snare the dancers). A grey, harmless steam which loiters around Siegfried's forge or the café in *La Bohème* is piped up direct from the house's boiler-room. Harmless too are the white drifts and pools created by hot water thrown over dry ice. Fanned low across the boards, they drift as swamp-mist through the death-scene of *Manon* and smooth out the bourréeing passage of Lady Lygon in *Enigma Variations*.

These visual conjuring-tricks are complemented by a battery of sound effects. The noises are prefabricated artificially on a synthesiser, which mingles basic notes and tones, or gained by treating natural sounds in a mixer, combining them and changing their frequency response. From their mixing-desk in a staff box close above the stage, they can assail the air from any point, or groan under the auditorium floorboards from amplifiers immured between the stalls and the staff canteen below. Other loudspeakers, circling the amphitheatre, lend a ghoulish ubiquity to the voice of the dragon Fafner as he dies in *Siegfried*, or send *The Ice Break*'s aeroplanes and police sirens jarring overhead.

Sometimes live noises – drums, thunder-sheets – are produced in distant rooms of the house and instantly transmitted through the mixing-desk in an amplified or distorted guise. Multiple gradations of pitch-change, delay and reverberation produce devils, in-

*Music staff discussing* Tosca *in rehearsal*

154

fernal winds, astral echoes and sepulchral voices – the thunder of *Otello* and the yelping of the *Der Freischütz* hellhounds. Even from the heart of the auditorium's dome ethereal choruses tremble in *Parsifal*; and *Siegfried*'s woodbird, standing with a repetiteur inside the cupola itself, sings down through a microphone with celestial strangeness.

As for the acting area itself, with its puny wings and octogenarian lifts, by the mid '80s work should be afoot to surround it with three subsidiary stages of equal size, ranged to its south, west and south-west. Electric motors will drive these stages along tracks on to the central acting area, complete with their scenery. But for the moment space is so cramped that it would be impossible concurrently to mount two such productions as, for instance, the prodigious *Ring* cycle produced by Götz Friedrich in 1974–6. This must take the stage alone. A flamboyant witness to the defeat of antiquated means by human inventiveness, its technical fulfilment, more than any other in the house's history, demanded that creation of the unprecedented which is the fascination and the headache of production for the stage.

Friedrich, a protégé of Felsenstein's *Welttheater*, saw the *Ring* not as Gothic fantasy but as an allegory of civilisation and its end, of how those who hold power corrupt and pervert the world. At its centre the designer Josef Svoboda conceived a giant platform mounted on a hydraulic piston-tower secured in the concrete foundations under the stage. Composed of elements bent from their natural purpose – the slew-ring of a building crane, five moog valves like those in America's Saturn rockets – this protean floor, thirty-seven foot square, transforms into mountain, cave, river. As it revolves, submerges or tilts into the sky, it becomes itself a protagonist in the drama, a symbol of primal energy, older than gods and men. At the cycle's beginning, when the universe is yet secure, it moves through only simple planes. Coated on its underside with thirty-six mirrors, it rises from the stage's sunken lifts to reflect the iridescent world of the Rhine Maidens, who cavort in a watery translucence of aquamarine and gold, turning cartwheels (these are dancers) or lolling on silver lamé air-mattresses under a river like champagne. When the great floor blossoms into a rainbow bridge leading the gods to Valhalla, each of the seven flights of wooden treads is kept horizontal by its own electric motor and pendulum beneath.

But as *Die Walküre* opens the next night, it does so on a platform whirling through darkness and coloured lights, its symmetry exploded by great gnarled rocks in a now disrupted world. Thereafter the pistoned stage lurches into angles and chasms. In *Siegfried*, as it swings Wotan into the sky, it opens up a gaping wound below, where Erda the earth goddess is entombed in the tubers of her ash tree and in eternal wisdom. Fifteen feet and an angle of forty degrees separate them, and the illusion is breathtaking.

The whole production, from its air-hung Valhalla to its six-foot Japanese lenses through which Hagen eavesdrops on his own manipulations, makes light of conventional space, until the platform settles at last, at the end of *Götterdämmerung* and the cyclic death of the world, to a sandy and level desolation. As for the dragon which Siegfried slays, with its central conning tower and sixteen claws each armoured like a Concorde's nose and each containing an actor, it comes slithering, slobbering and clanking over the stage in a paroxysm of lights – a great dishevelled senility of a dragon which is less a homogeneous creature than a mindless swarm of evil.

On an opera's first night, all such spectacle leaves the sphere of the production

*Chorus dressing-room*

manager and passes into that of the technical department. Fifty-six stage hands and twenty-eight electricians work a three-day week in two tough shifts from eight o'clock in the morning until eleven at night, often running into the small hours and overtime. They operate in a close antiphony, the stage hands generally preceding the electricians, who must focus their lights on assembled scenery. Once or twice a week they may strip out the evening show into the early hours and start to build the sets for the morning rehearsal, often tumbling into sleep in their rest area or sprawled out in the green room before returning on stage a few hours later.

About a quarter of these men come from families employed in stage business for generations – old Holborn and Covent Garden clans addicted to their bizarre night-life. They work in a blustery camaraderie – shifts 'A' and 'B' vilifying one another in ribald graffiti left scrawled on the backs of scenery. No straight theatre demands such tough hours or the manhandling of such heavy and elaborate sets. Even the scene-changes, which often synchronise with the orchestra, must be effected with a special precision and silence. As the curtain descends on the twenty-second interval of music which transforms the death-pond of *Wozzeck* to a bawdy beer-garden, the crew must rush away a bench, signpost and stretch of reeds, fly in the walls and roof of the seedy tavern, and convene a bar complete with piano, tables, stools, chairs, glasses and drinks, where twenty people lounge. The conductor, if the green bulb on his rostrum fails to light up on time, sustains a longer-than-usual drum roll. So hairline is the timing, that when a stage hand caught his fingers in the lid of the piano, he disrupted the whole opening because he stopped and shook them in pain for two seconds.

After performance, these men clear the sets with the same hypnotic speed. The blossom-laden trellises and screen-built house of *Madama Butterfly* are swept away in half an hour. Even the heavy, raked stage for *Peter Grimes* begins to flake like a rotten skin as the stage hands swarm over it the moment the curtain falls. Everything happens at the run. As the bar for the white backcloth is lowered, ten men converge along its length. It is hitched and tied and rises with a long, soprano whine into the grid. Seven big stage hands at a time wrestle the heavier boards on to iron stage-trucks in a tempest of uninventive swearing, and the underlying rostra are collapsed and stacked in the wings or piled on to the trucks and rumbled to the mouth of a lift.

Meanwhile, in a cacophany of shouting between stage and gallery flymen, they are hanging the palace railings of *Don Giovanni*. Four or five suspended bars are filled at a time: some with cloths, others with lamps. Within thirty minutes the ramped stage has been chopped away and the electricians are checking their circuits and changing colour filters in preparation for the more delicate focusing of lamps next morning. A quarter of an hour later, the place is empty.

The slow-moving lift, which is the main conduit of scenery through the house, lowers its burden with tantalising caution out of the south wing and into the scenery depot of Floral Hall, an old vegetable emporium acquired by the opera house in 1977, soon after the removal of Covent Garden market. In the tranquil spaces of its steel and glass conservatory, whose porticoes lift to a roof twittering with sparrows, the scenery for running productions is massed in unrecognisable and exorcised heaps– dismembered palace battlements, slivers of anonymous interiors, isolated columns and cliff-faces, stairs to nowhere. Here and there looms a canopied throne or the huge, sorrowful elephant heads from *L'Africaine*; or a wood and canvas carriage, its wheels padded for noiselessness, glitters with gilt and *trompe l'œil* paint.

On a show's last night the sets may be transported from the opera house altogether by the 'outside gang' of eight, who accompany lorries packed with scenery to warehouses at King's Cross or Kent. They leave from Floral Hall and from the stage's opposite wing, where stairs descend direct into the street and where a slatted ramp padded with coconut matting gives passage to animals. Horses homely and horses aristocratic, donkeys and fractious goats and a Highland cow from *Moses and Aaron* – all come prancing or lumbering up by this entrance. Jittery *Der Rosenkavalier* whippets and patrician *Don Carlos* wolf-hounds enter by the stage door. Some have proved quite unmusical. The hens which interrupted arias in the tavern scene of *Boris Godunov* discreetly disappeared, and the *Der Rosenkavalier* monkey was exiled after an unplanned bout of diarrhoea.

Even while a performance is moving towards its opening night, the average evening is occupied by one of a giant cavalcade of revivals. The maintenance or resuscitation of this inheritance – a production's life fluctuates around twenty years – is the day-to-day business of the house. An uncomplicated opera, recently performed, can be remounted in four days; a thoroughly revised production may receive six weeks; and although rehearsal time for revivals is uniquely generous by opera standards, almost all proceed with a swiftness which would terrify an actor in straight theatre.

The principals know their parts already – both how they will sing and act them. There is rarely time to change a used and familiar characterisation. The new conductor's concept of the music may be utterly different from his predecessor's. As for the producer, he must create what alchemy he can from all these forgone ingredients, and must maintain – or even strengthen – that elusive inner energy which was once the production's heart.

No revival can embalm the past, without itself being dead; but the furniture and architecture of many sets almost dictate where a singer will stand or walk. In studio rehearsal the whole of Zeffirelli's Act I set for *Tosca*, with its vistas of aisle and transept radiating through incense-misted vaults, its votive lamps and kicking cupids and altar-screen – all were marked by three dilapidated chairs and a few props pulled out of a whisky box. Among such musty focal points, the producer must not only rediscover the production's first impetus, but try to invent anew, exploiting the qualities of the singers assigned to him. Grace Bumbry, rehearsing *Tosca*, suddenly cried out: 'I don't see the point of crossing the stage here! It doesn't work!' What was right for Maria Callas is wrong for her – and so the moment goes on living.

New productions do not inexorably decay. Sometimes, on the contrary, they only reach maturity in revival, when the producer's original ideas are developed to the full. In other cases the whole heart of a failing opera may eventually undergo transplant in a 'revised production'; while other stagings, like Everding's *Die Zauberflöte*, invite many choices in development, so that each revival emerges different. But to attempt the reanimation of others, of course, is like giving a blood transfusion to a corpse: nothing happens at all. With the planned collusion of the original conductor and producer gone, the chorus's motivation faded in a language foreign to them, with the stars arriving and departing in their set interpretations, with the scenery dating or decaying and a staff producer retrieving another man's concepts – in all these the spark of life must eventually dim.

Even revivals of ballet, protected as they are by the cohesion of the company, and often by their own choreographer, can follow a similar graph. For a while they may reach a standstill which sometimes – as in Ashton's *La Fille Mal Gardée* or *Cinderella* – looks like the stasis of perfection. But then the precision of scene-changes and the focusing of lights starts unnoticeably to falter, and far later the dancers on whose bodies a work was created are superseded by others, and there may come a feeling of losing ground, talk of how to revitalise, comparisons with a past already unassessable.

The fight to maintain the ballet classics is above all a physical one. They are rejuvenated not only for their own sake, but as the gauge and guardian of technical excellence. Stage rehearsals (generally limited to three with piano and one with orchestra) continue in a storm of criticism and rebuke. Leotards, leggings, flounced skirts and jeans replace in rehearsal the moonlit Taglioni dresses of *Les Sylphides*. The unlit auditorium is hushed with teaching staff and in mid-dance the irascible voice of Michael Somes, amplified by microphone, erupts out of the darkness: 'Go out more, Sally! . . . Farther in, Julie! . . . Stay in your place, Eagling!'

Poised in the wings, a crowd of small, enclosed and sometimes beautiful faces – waiting, or second casts – gazes at the stage through balletic cats' eyes, and seems, in its Degas repose, to be without motive or muscle. But as the last ensemble finishes, the staff descends. Somes, Larsen, Gregory, the ballet master converge on them in a fusillade of censure and reprimand. The whole performance, they imply, was a perpetual eyesore, without flow, without line, without symmetry, without anything at all. 'You're never in line!' Somes barks at a pale, clenched face. 'Never once! Never once in line! What's wrong? Yesterday you were all right. Today your head was wrong from the beginning! Just look in the mirror and see. You're doing it like this' – he inclines his head – 'absolutely wrong!' He swoops on a coryphée. 'Why the arabesque? I told you yesterday I want you to dream it. Let it drift. Don't go jerking your legs.'

'It's very difficult,' she murmers.

But now Larsen advances in support. 'And you moved your arm across your face.' She turns to Somes. 'She was dreadful.'

The face stares back at them, crumpled, tough. She tries the step again.

'No,' adds Gregory. 'Your head is still too low. It should be there' – she moves it four inches higher. 'And you ended up too far downstage.'

For ten or fifteen minutes the voices ascend in a black cloud of retribution. Sins of omission and inclusion, minute slips and unforgivable derelictions pile up like a Last Judgement. 'You haven't understood a *thing*, have you? . . . at least five inches. . . . I don't know what made you do it . . . a full split-second. . . .'

The sylphides disintegrate into woebegone groups, or engage in stricken little dances of their own, practising again. The staff fall to complaining among themselves. 'Why weren't they doing it right? They were awful. . . . They're faceless, they don't use their eyes . . . That lovely *chassé* – ruined. . . .'

In no art is grace more dearly bought. The illusion of earthless ease in Ashton's ballets conceals a furnace of struggle. That classic of abstract dance, *Symphonic Variations*, whose steps seem as natural as the music made flesh, was the result of more painstaking revision than any other of his works, and is an eighteen-minute marathon to perform. Its three girls and three men occupy no worldly time or space. Cooled by white costumes and a pale green backcloth, they float and reform in a galactic mystery, and seem of an essence with the air which they inhabit. The music pours itself away in a rippling soliloquy. The men soar and twirl with unearthly grace, and the girls glide in their arms, carried low like

*Moments before dancing the Hostess in* Les Biches, *Marguerite Porter waits in a prop room of the wings, while a wardrobe assistant repairs her dress*

drifting elements of the music. Then they part in a leaping or shimmering crescent, the orchestra bursts into celebration and they run with linked hands, spin, jump, arabesque, and return at last to the statuesque tranquillity from which they came.

Yet viewed close in rehearsal, the dancers in this lyric dream reveal a terrible strain. Once or twice the men shout pleas or orders to one another, their bodies racked by gasps; and the girls let out sharp cries for breath. Their proper placement one to another is so exact that the smallest imprecision glares out. The effortless-looking steps exacerbate any physical weakness, and may fill the bodies of both girls and men with a wincing pain.

At the end Michael Somes, who is the guardian of this cruel and ravishing ballet (he danced with Fonteyn in its 1946 premiere) arrives on the stage uncharacteristically pleased, followed by Ashton. The dancers surround them in a rasping semicircle, pouring sweat from their foreheads and backs, the magic disintegrated. The shaven tips of the girls' shoes are black with grime, their hair dripping under the tiaras. Ashton, forever seeking the aesthetic, indicates their hips. 'You should *bend* more, *bend*.'

The pain repeats itself in *Dances of Albion, Voluntaries*, parts of *The Firebird*, of *The Rite of Spring, Les Noces* and many others. During performances of Ashton's *Rhapsody*, the anguished cries on stage are shrouded from the audience by the curtain of orchestral sound rising between. After the first few minutes the jewelled headdresses and apricot skirts and leotards are clothing a human sacrifice, the ethereally smiling faces already oozing sweat, the gracefully held shoulders secretly in labour. As they gain the wings (only to return sixty seconds later) their *bourrées* wither into limps, the smiles drop off, the bodies sag forward from the hips and they breathe in hoarse gusts and whistling bursts of air.

*Stage doorman clears a path for Baryshnikov*

One of the *corps* is massaging her ankles and mewling to herself in a musical sing-song.
'You should have been in the opera,' another says.
'Yes. Oh God. *Yes, yes.*'
In the opposite wing, clearly heard across the stage's breadth, another girl is howling with agony, grasping her calves. Even Lesley Collier, at the last, moans and cries softly to herself, clasping her shoulders, and a moment later returns to the stage smiling, athletically soubrette, only the faintest throb of her breast betraying her. As the curtain descends the dancers slump like marionettes. The instant before it goes up again their faces lift, light and smile. The audience, unaware of what it is exacting, goes on with its applause, and the dancers continue to droop and shine alternately with the curtain's fall and rise, in a macabre etiquette of grace and suffering.

They accept a degree of pain extraordinary in everyday life. The body becomes a map of ravages and susceptibilities. The girls dance unflinching through their menstrual periods. In the longer classics it becomes second nature to break through the pain barrier, and to exercise an injured muscle rather than transfer the strain to another part of the body. In performance they swear less frequently, but more horribly, than the opera chorus; and even away from it, they perhaps bring more strain to the difficult choreography of life.

Rather as a musical singer, who anticipates the shape of a phrase before he sings it, will find his breathing fall naturally into place, so the musical dancer shapes and breathes the dance phrase. But for most others, caught up in the Herculean labours of technique, the music's beauty is reduced to a mass of notes and time-values, and certain of them run into torment through sheer lack of oxygen. Some dancers go on counting the choreographic bars out loud even on stage, and many more will be counting internally. In difficult ballets this discipline is so ingrained that at a dress rehearsal of *The Rite of Spring*, when the string section of a visiting orchestra missed an entry, the voices of the *corps* rose in immediate unison, chanting their bars like a rhythmic spell.

**Rhapsody.** Frederick Ashton choreographing with ballet master Christopher Newton, Mikhail Baryshnikov and Lesley Collier

**Rhapsody**. Frederick Ashton directing a rehearsal from the stalls, with Christopher Newton and The Royal Ballet's artistic administrator, Iris Law

**Rhapsody.** For the world première at the Queen Mother's eightieth birthday gala, a special box is assembled in the grand tier. Cleaners take a break, and Royal Box attendants put the finishing touches to one another

Top: arrival of the royal party; left: Frederick Ashton and Norman Morrice on stage with Lesley Collier before the curtain rises on *Rhapsody*; above: John Tooley is called to the Crush Bar telephone

**Rhapsody**. Mikhail Baryshnikov in performance, Lesley Collier in the wings, and Sir Frederick Ashton at curtain call

**Rhapsody**. After the performance the company, led by
Frederick Ashton, applauds the Queen Mother, who has
moved to the Royal Box before attending a brief reception
on stage, together with Princess Margaret. Bottom right:
Mikhail Baryshnikov with Dame Marie Rambert

**Der Ring des Nibelungen**. Beneath the stage, technical director Tom Macarthur and his staff inspect the hydraulic piston-tower which supports the pivoting platform. Bottom: in the shadow of the platform, the stage elevators are lowered around a column of glittering lenses which will become Alberich's control-tower in *Das Rheingold* Opposite: producer Götz Friedrich at a stage rehearsal, above; John Dobson (Mime) standing on the lip of the platform, Alberto Remedios (Siegfried) celebrating the forging of the magic sword

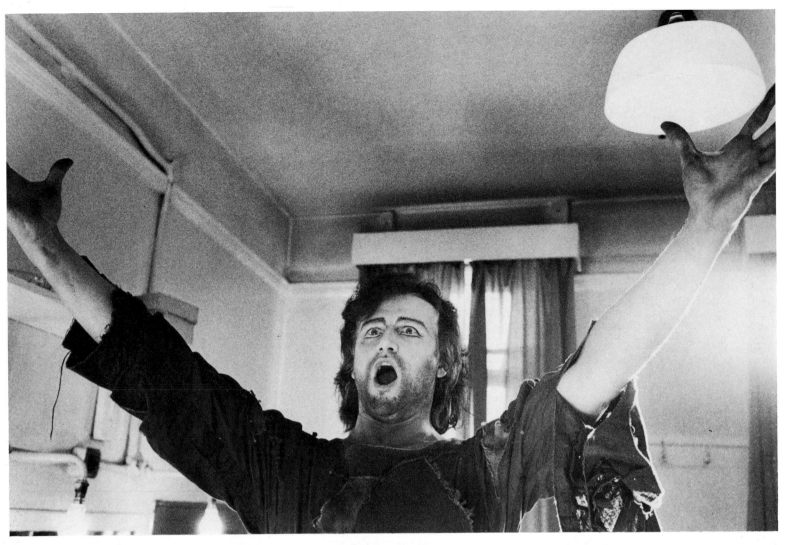

**Der Ring des Nibelungen** backstage. Peter Hofmann (Siegmund) in his dressing-room, Valkyries warming up their voices in the backstage chorus room, and Donald McIntyre (Wanderer) anxious about the acoustic effects of his hat. Opposite: Matti Salminen (Fafner) leaves his dressing-room for the stage

**Der Ring des Nibelungen**. Opposite above: Donner forges the rainbow bridge to Valhalla at the end of *Das Rheingold*. Below: the Wanderer journeys through the forests in search of Mime

Brünnhilde's sleep

Overleaf: *Die Walküre*. Donald McIntyre (Wotan), Berit Lindholm (Brünnhilde) in rehearsal

**Hamlet** in revival. Robert Helpmann returns to supervise the ballet which he premiered in 1942, in Leslie Hurry's haunting set. Anthony Dowell (Hamlet) rehearses with Marguerite Porter (Ophelia), opposite top. Helpmann advises Monica Mason (the Queen), opposite left, and consults Frederick Ashton, near left. Below: Anthony Dowell and Graham Fletcher (Gravedigger)

**Otello**. Below: Placido Domingo in the shadow of Iago

Opposite: Ande Anderson, Sir John Tooley and the
wardrobe director, debating a point of dress with Placido
Domingo; Carlos Kleiber and John Tooley on the set; and
the offstage trumpets for Act III

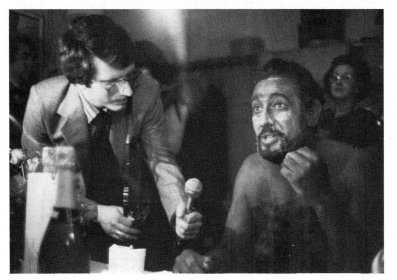

**Otello** behind the set. Children's coach Jean Povey, top, hidden by scenery, encourages her children as they face the audience to sing their hymn to Desdemona; above: as Otello enters Desdemona's bedchamber, stage manager Peter Morrell closes the door unseen behind him. Left: Placido Domingo gives a radio interview as he removes his makeup after the first night

**Tosca**. Shirley Verrett receives a final touch of makeup in the wings and is conducted through Tosca's offstage cantata in Act II
Opposite: Act III. An assistant stage manager waits for Tosca to jump from the castle battlements onto a prearranged bed

# PERFORMANCE

An hour before performance, the stage falls eerily silent. The electricians have focused the last lamps and the scenery is set. The tiers of the auditorium are banked in blazing but empty semicircles of light. The centre of activity and nerves has shifted to the dressing-rooms, where wardrobe assistants have been laying out costumes since early afternoon.

Dancers arrive long before singers do. Two hours before a performance, their dressing-rooms are already filling up, and their lockers disgorging a miscellany of pointe shoes, cosmetics, corn-plasters, wig glue, mascots, fake curls, chocolates, hair dryers. An acrid smell of greasepaint and shampoo starts to permeate the air, and under their long mirrors the counters become scattered with fans or tiaras.

Many dancers feel a security in arriving early. Jennifer Penney reaches the house at three o'clock for a 7.30 performance carrying six pairs of pointe shoes which she trims, slices and stitches into order, dulling their shine and scraping their soles. For half an hour she ceremoniously lays out her makeup, wigs and hairpins, then sits facing a spreading litter of coffee-cups and mangoes, listening to the radio, before another three-quarters of an hour pass in making up her face to a porcelain finish. At six o'clock she tentatively warms up, performing the steps which most worry her in a gentle ritual of self-assurance. But by this time the dressing-rooms are restless with the comings and goings of wardrobe assistants, and the atmosphere of the house trembling with a faint disquiet. In the sub-aqueous silence of the green room, the only nerveless figure may be Kenneth MacMillan, fast asleep on a sofa with his feet crossed, like a Crusader on his tomb.

As for the singers, the principals arrive about an hour before curtain-up, and the chorus later still, roistering down the gaunt passageways to their new dressing-rooms. The visiting stars, whom many foreign houses coddle and humour, are treated here with a rather formal kindness and a British distrust of tantrum. In the dressing-rooms, gazing into the merciless mirrors under tungsten light, the wigmaster or his assistants blend the foreign stars' makeup to their characterisation and costumes. Smoothing the skin in greasepaint or water-based 'pancake' powdered firm, they adapt the make-up to counter-act the vivid stage-light, shading away the jowls, opening up the eyes, highlighting the cheekbones. The dancers and British singers make up alone. To project in so large a theatre, especially for the constant movement of ballet, the features may be exaggerated into a Kabuki grotesquerie, or a face rebuilt by a new play of emphases and neutral shading to achieve the well-shaped mouth, level eyebrows and clear-cut cheekbones of the classic ballerina.

In the communal dressing-rooms, amidst a wholesale spraying of hair and glueing of wigs and blending of eyeshadow, a nervous camaraderie develops. Singers swop lipsticks; dancers help glue on each other's eyelashes. It is during these moments, as they watch their faces grow strange to them in the mirror, that some artists think themselves into the character they are about to portray. David Wall starts assuming many of his roles at such a time, after mentally rehearsing their technical problems before an afternoon nap; but Monica Mason works herself gently into her part all day. Singers as disparate as Donald McIntyre and Katia Ricciarelli, provided they resolve a character powerfully in rehearsal, do not prepare themselves at all, but find its emotional charge arrive unbidden as they step on stage; and Janet Baker, who likes a new role to mature in her for a full year, hates even to begin rehearsals without the character as her second nature.

Through the dressing-rooms, inescapably, and into the smallest office, the loud-speakers transmit the stage manager's alerts: half an hour, quarter of an hour before curtain-up. Some artists fall unnaturally silent. Others start to chatter obsessively. Little superstitions appear. They mutter shibboleths, kiss mascots, try out little songs or dances for good luck. Doreen Wells used to touch the passage walls with either foot in a cabbalistic ritual of her own, as she walked to the stage. Lesley Collier refuses to have new shoes laid on her dressing-room counter.

Some roles have the scent of fear about them. On an evening of *Les Noces* or *The Rite of Spring*, the *corps de ballet* becomes a patchwork of tense quietness or frenetic gossip, and a performance of *Swan Lake* touches them with unease all day. Some singers have been physically sick before going on stage. Others engage in deep breathing exercises or prac-tise yawning to relax the throat muscles. A few will sing through their whole role in the dressing-rooms out of pure nerves.

But most restrict themselves to a few exercises for the placing of the voice, and for a

while their warbled bars and octaves mingle faintly along the corridors. The dancers limber up for ten or twenty minutes in the studios, in their dressing-rooms or under the pallid working lights on stage. They like to begin relaxed, a little tired. But even here they differ. Wayne Eagling prefers to start almost cold, whereas Stephen Jefferies, who suffers low blood pressure, works off his surplus tension and self-consciousness by levering himself up to a furious aggression, especially for his explosive entries in *La Fille Mal Gardée* or *Daphnis and Chloë*. Sometimes, half an hour before curtain-up, the ballet master or his assistant conduct a 'placing' session on stage – a schematic rehearsal of the opening *corps*, perhaps, or an ensemble to integrate a last-minute substitute. Around them the theatre is still quiet, apparently uninhabited, the curtain down and no sound penetrating from beyond, unless a player is practising alone in its silence.

But in their medley of rooms around the pit mezzanine the orchestra members are already attuning their lips to the mouthpieces of brass, the string players kneading their fingers, the woodwind warming their reeds, and in the foyer the audience assembling. One by one, from the coffin-like ranks of the double-basses and a storeroom of 'cellos nearby, or from the clinical restrooms for woodwind and strings, the players filter into the pit. The noise of the audience swirls and sighs around them now like a troubled and invisible sea. Beyond and above them, the cream and gold crescents of the auditorium seem to rise as one close-layered scarp, in whose foreshortened dimness the people's faces mill and coalesce far away. Sunk low, the players feel like fish in a pool, exposed but unseen. The blue saucer of the dome swims overhead in a parody of sky. They tune up on the oboe, or switch on an electronic note 'A' beneath the conductor's rostrum. Occasion-

*The orchestra tuning up*

ally a few spectators peer over the rim of the orchestra rail; and high above the pit's ends, adrift and puppet-like, a line of box-occupants idly trains its opera glasses down.

Behind the curtain, five minutes before the start of a ballet, the stage fills up with dancers. For twenty minutes they have been coming and going over its boards in a silent and desultory build-up, and now they congregate all together, trying steps, complaining of injuries, sometimes almost unrecognisable in their make-up. They talk quietly, nervously together. Underfoot the stage is taped with little guiding crosses and arrows, which they rarely use. No sound percolates from the auditorium. Members of the staff – Morrice, Somes, Gregory, Larsen, Newton – move talking among them or stand facing them with their backs to the curtains – curtains which are scarred on the inside by the crimson-lined double curve of the cables which draw them back. The conductor comes backstage and talks momentarily with the dancers. Sometimes a principal asks him to slow or speed a passage of the music, but although he nods sympathetically, he senses that the dancer has simply needed reassurance.

Then the working lamps go off. Beyond the curtain the orchestra can be heard throbbing and whining to itself like a chasm-full of trolls. The staff slips away into the auditorium, and the dancers vanish from the boards, which blossom into lights as the opening cast assembles. On the televisions around the proscenium the conductor can be seen mounting his rostrum. The audience clapping sounds muffled and unreal like water clattering over stones. Then the curtains part.

For the dancer, they rise from a stage self-contained in its own brightness. The terror of its exposure is made bearable by the merging of the audience into a collective darkness,

*Frederica von Stade with the prompter*

pricked only by blue lights above the exits. In ballet the wings are rarely overshadowed by high-built scenery. They stretch in thin glades of intersplashed light and blackness, where electric cables dribble like trip-wires and the dancers – especially during some admired solo or *pas de deux* – fill the shadows in jewelled and exotic shoals among free-standing lamps which shine almost at eye level. The wings are the conduit between fantasy and reality. They belong to neither. Exiled princesses and swan-maidens stitch pointe shoes in their darkness. Stagehands stand joking twenty feet from an incendiary *pas de deux*. The recesses rustle with limbering figures; sometimes a member of a second cast imitates the movements of the first in a ghostly counterpoint, or the *corps* sweeps in from the stage in a flood of evaporated tension. But the atmosphere is intimate, only mutedly nervous – a concourse of highly-trained friends. They gossip and laugh quietly behind the safety of orchestral sound. The mood of the huge, excited audience, with its portentous criticism and vaunted inside knowledge, is far away.

Sometimes three or four scenic flats are drawn together into an offstage cubicle where a table, a cracked mirror and a blue lamp create a pool of sordid secrecy for some lightning costume-change. Certain transmutations, like those in *Marguerite and Armand*, must be completed in less than thirty seconds. The principals dash into the cubicles or props rooms on either side and stand like shop-window mannequins while the wardrobe master and two or three dressers transform them.

Backstage, during intervals, it is costume-changing again which consumes time. The intervals can abstract the dancers, cauterise their energies. There is no real rest. In the canteen the ubiquitous loudspeakers nag on: 'Principal ladies' dresser, would you come to the stage, please, bringing a spare feather for the Firebird, thank you. . . . Actors for Scene Two – Monsters – this is your call. Monsters. . . .' And the Monsters tramp up flights of gloomy stairs from their steamy communal dressing-rooms.

On the opening night of a newly-created ballet, everything – lighting, costume-changes, even the stage manager's voice on the tannoy – is touched by a new uncertainty. The moments before the curtain-up, and before the staff leave the dancers for the auditorium, are pregnant with fear and a sense almost of valediction. The dancers feel an awesome responsibility to the choreographer, and he to them. He offers fleeting advice and encouragement, and kisses them. It is as if they will meet again only a long time hence. After the ballet begins the wings remain thick with dancers who would normally be in their dressing-rooms, now waiting long before their cues, gazing wide-eyed into the arena. The audience in its silence becomes a threatening enigma. They wait for its voice. They have lived with the ballet so long in its making that they may feel half blind to it, and that the first cool perception of the audience – a comfortless first-night blend of socialite and balletomane – will tell them the truth. Meanwhile, the choreographer – the man who has set in motion this spectacle so expensive in spirit and means – is sitting in an inconspicuous row of the grand tier, waiting to hear the distaste, delight or indifference of the crowd enfolding him, and perhaps the insincerities of his friends.

Nervous or assured, the dances unroll for judgement. Some have scarcely evolved since their creation. Others, in feeling, are unrecognisably changed. The lantern solo of *Isadora*, which began fluent and beautiful in the studio, is now danced by a red-haired and lascivious Merle Park as a futile antic – intentional pastiche. By the tarnished light of an old gas-lamp, she succumbs into a Bacchic revel of air-flailing arms and legs, a parody of her past, her technique rotted away.

# PERFORMANCE

The first, warm breaths of applause bring momentary relief. The audience is probably unsure. It does not know where to clap or laugh, what to expect. But to the dancers it seems to lie like a unified monster in the darkness. As the final curtain descends the whole cast is massed in the wings to hear its judgement. For ballets in which they fervently believe, a euphoria like a bonfire rises and glows among the dancers as the applause goes on. The stage manager bellows their curtain-calls above the din – principals, choreographer, designer, conductor. The monster roars. As the spotlit principals stand before the curtain in a rain of flowers, the *corps* hangs back behind it, still in formation, and breaks into laughter and exclamations as the cheers continue. The audience's exhilaration is sustained and orchestrated by the curtain-calls of the dancers. Again and again the curtain lifts on an incandescent rain of applause, dampens it to a drizzle as it descends, detonates it again as it rises. Bouquets are heaped at the ballerinas' feet, piled into their arms. Suddenly, backstage, everybody is kissing everybody else (or nearly); around the dressing-rooms the tiny passageways are congested with friends; and long after the audience has gone the staff, guests and dancers are talking and embracing on the stage in a flotsam of trampled carnations.

But the choreographer, however elated, feels, in the end, a deprivation. MacMillan wakes up the next morning still worrying about a ballet which is suddenly beyond recall. Ashton experiences an acute sense of loss and never wants to hear the music again. A sense of *déjà vu* engulfs him. 'Sometimes I feel as if I'm ploughing up the same row of dirt. Then I think, O God, why can't a miracle take place, why can't I think of something really astonishing, something really new – and that depresses me. All the dancing is speaking my same old language.'

The choreographer, of course, does not see his new work clearly for a while. If it survives in the repertoire, it may be subjected to his prunings and slashings long after its first night. And this ironic lack of objectivity is not confined to him. The singer only hears his own voice accurately when recorded, the dancer cannot witness his own dancing. Even when lit for performance, the stage scenery may convince an audience, but never the performers who inhabit it. They must fulfil an illusion which they cannot share. They dance in a picture. To the audience of *The Sleeping Beauty*, Lesley Collier arrives radiant between Palladian arcades in a garden of elysian magic. They see columns, trees, vistas – a background palace of airy stateliness. But in fact, riven by nerves, she mounts a rough wooden platform ('It's like a call to the scaffold') and runs on to stage between cobwebby hangings of paper-thin pillars, half blinded by an eye-level lamp on the far side. The painted palace hangs an arm's length behind her. The music of whose beauty she must be the expression is a slave-driver refusing her rest, and she imagines the sweat already coursing through her makeup.

Nerves grow worse with age when the dancer has a reputation to lose. Some never go on stage without a quaking of the heart. Antoinette Sibley feels tense for a week before every performance; and even Collier thinks her formidable technique pitifully frail: 'Even if I'm not performing in *Sleeping Beauty*, but I'm in the theatre and hear that entrance-music playing for somebody else, I feel sick in anticipation for them.'

On the evening of an opera premiere, the chorus bursting through the stage door may be confronted by a profusion of last-minute reminders on its notice-board – the producer invoking moods and motives, the staff producer stressing vital cues, the stage manager pleading that they remove their wrist-watches and cheerful socks – notices all greeted with a salvo of racy or cynical comments. The chorus's bonhommie survives into canteen snacks before the show and erupts again in the intervals when their Dionysian revelry spills blamelessly into the green room. Five minutes before curtain-up the names of those who are absent are broadcast over the tannoy, like a bulletin of the disgraced in some proletarian state.

But once in the wings, all this robust anarchy dwindles to a sturdy quiet. The singers stand backstage with a calm ballast, and restrict their limbering to faint, throat-clearing notes. Compared to the competitive fraternity of the ballet, with its rarified blend of adolescence and discipline, these sobered crowds seem middle-aged, easier, limned together by casual friendships and the common bond of the voice. The cliff-like scenery and built-up boards of many operas turn the flashing chiaroscuro of the ballet wings into black and looming defiles, where the chorus moves in slow clusters beside an invisible stage. Far back, the whole area opens on to a dark void. Here the cleft floor of the paint studio hangs in twin slivers of light, and the rope-hung fly galleries are suspended high up like organ lofts in a cathedral.

The easy-going and multi-national singers need strong stage management. Assistants with scores and winking torches cue on both stars and chorus from the wings, and usher them off dark sets by the light of the safety lamps. The stage manager is a roving, super-vising, checking presence. After each interval she escorts the conductor out of his rest-room and through the iron doors of the orchestra pit. His presence on the opera stage is pervasive. Touched by a Rembrandt glow from the light of his lectern, his baton is the

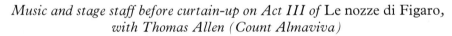

*Music and stage staff before curtain-up on Act III of* Le nozze di Figaro, *with Thomas Allen (Count Almaviva)*

focus of the singer's eye. In a blurr of refracted lights and shadows, he appears on the televisions for the offstage bands, and the principals themselves, as they poise in the wings, may be watching him on a stage assistant's screen.

But when the singer steps on stage he is alone with his voice, and its first note strikes him always as a tiny miracle. For the singing voice is as vulnerable and unnatural as the dancing body. Throat, chest, shoulders, jaw – all the organs of tone and resonance – must sing out unrestrained. But the diaphragm needs tension. Carrying this complex despot of a voice into a first night debut, clothed in strange dress in an unfamiliar set, he can experience himself no more objectively than the dancer can. He cannot even hear the true balance of his voice with the orchestra. He must judge it by experience and by what he has been told. His impact stems not only from himself, but from conductor, producer, designer and the shadowy hosts of others serving them.

As she enters the tall gates which dominate *Macbeth*, the sleepwalking Renata Scotto grips the heart before ever she sings. A single lamp, set high backstage, pierces them with a beam of disembodied whiteness, which freezes the steps below to an icy cascade. She comes in a tattered black gown, holding a guttering candle. As the music shimmers and agitates around her, she descends in a tunnel of moonlight – she is both sleeping and mad. Her shadow precedes her like a snake down the steps. Her hair hangs lustreless and dishevelled around a greenish skull of face. It is ravished and lost. Whitened by greasepaint, the full cheeks hollowed grey, the eyes blackened around their sockets, her features are those of a decadent child, its senses loosened. Light, music, movement, makeup, design – all conspire for a few irreducible moments in her floating desolation.

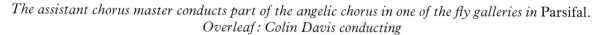

*The assistant chorus master conducts part of the angelic chorus in one of the fly galleries in* Parsifal.
*Overleaf: Colin Davis conducting*

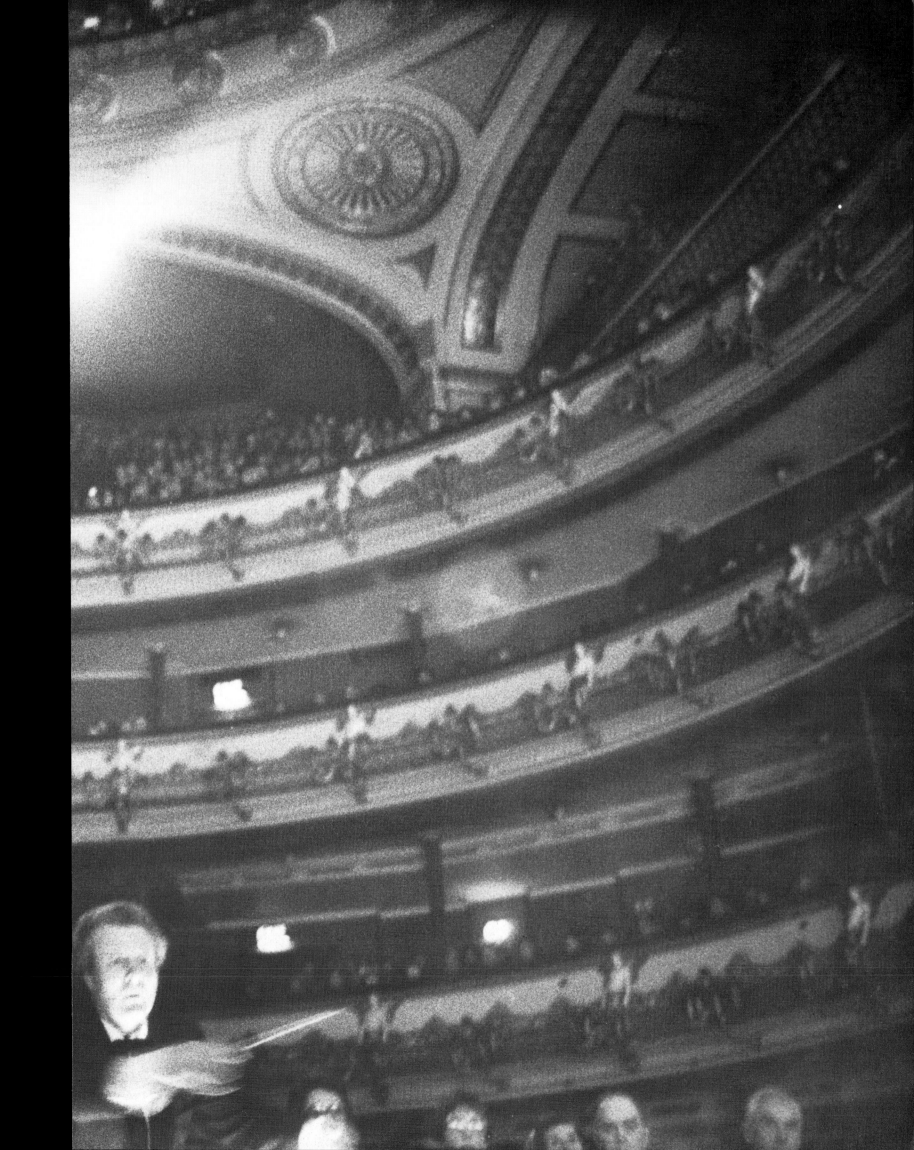

They conspire, too, to heighten *Don Giovanni*'s end. In its green palace porticoes, the conclave of devotional statues (chopped-up dummies, insulating rope, butter muslin) hovers above the swerving stairway. Time is running out. Ruggero Raimondi, his scarlet jerkin slashed open in lascivious bravado, ready for Hell, awaits his avenging guest with neurotic courtesies to the thin air. Above him the vortex of the designer's stair intimates a spiral up to heaven or a corkscrew into purgatory. Then the Commendatore appears at the stair's head. The music swirls supernaturally beneath him. The horror and buffoonery of Richard Van Allan's Leporello ends in abrupt violence as Raimondi hurls him through a screen (Van Allan secretly padded in rubberised carpet). High on the stair, Raimondi ascends and clasps the statue's hand. Fire bathes the walls. The Hell-mouth gapes. In a room near the staff canteen the chorus master and fourteen basses, with a closed-circuit television and fish-pole microphone, send up a pulsing demons' chorus and pray that nobody smashes a dish in the nearby kitchens. Fractionally delayed in the sound engineer's mixing-desk, their singing vibrates with an unearthly hollowness. On stage, as Raimondi tumbles half the length of the stairs, the terrible chorus and deepening flames engulf him, and the porticoes meet around the smoke-filled circle of Hell.

The flunkeys run to seal the final curtains. John Tooley and Colin Davis, the artistic administrator and the production manager, crowd the stage with the singers. Behind the house curtain, the 'reds' frontcloth is dropped in to isolate the principals in spotlit crimson. There is the same tense listening to the monster spread in the dimness – to the shades of its voice as singers, producer, designer, conductor take their curtain-calls. But while the premiere of a ballet emits a cloud of anxious hope, the first night of an opera sees

*Stage flunkeys, in uniforms given by Buckingham Palace*

more diffused and unravellable concerns: the prestige of the house and the honour of the composer, the esteem of individual singers, of conductor, of producer.

In no opera house is the response of the audience more cherished by the international stars. Singers to whom the claques and screaming of Italian houses are almost a commonplace speak of a Covent Garden ovation with special delight. The audience does not leap to its feet as at the Metropolitan, or let out the heart-stricken cries of the Bolshoi and Kirov. It has the British warm-coolness. Temperate, self-effacing, it is, in its way, rather sensitive. Its respectful silence – calculated at only fifty decibel, a whisper – is rarely broken in mid-performance. Its applause is often dutiful, and occasionally so tepidly charitable that one Continental singer swears she would prefer booing. But in ballet, now and then, it crackles into clapping in the middle of a solo – disrupting or spurring on its dancer – and after certain operas (such as *Elektra* and *Falstaff*) it may settle to a long, warm thunder. It is almost never unkind. A type of grateful, measured final applause entrenches everybody in his seat for eight or ten minutes. And rarely, there is a moment when the curtain falls in silence on an audience too moved, for a second, to speak.

The reserved response from the body of the house partly stems from its seat allocation. A central area of orchestra stalls, together with almost all the grand tier boxes, is bought by business firms on a premium scheme. The apparent internationalism of music and dance provides ideal entertainment for foreign business guests. In exchange for top payments – a huge guarantee to the box office – these companies buy seats on a regular basis throughout the season, and accept opera or ballet equally. Even so, unsold places sometimes remain in the stalls, and may pass to schools and clubs at concessionary rates, with priority to the regions and the young.

High above, deep beyond the golden friezes and lunettes of the ceiling, the 600-seat amphitheatre is filled by a more constant and more enthusiastic audience. For all its personality-worship, it is often keenly knowledgeable. It has come for the performance, not for the occasion. On many ballet nights it shows a preponderance of women; on opera, sometimes, a slight imbalance of men. In its topmost reaches Winnie Pradier, the oldest serving employee of the house (she came in 1934) holds genial court behind a bar bright with mugs of her own flowers, and all around, the *aficionados* argue over the merits of previous casts, and music students occupy lit lecterns high in the upper slips.

Nobody perceives these audience distinctions more sharply than the front-of-house personnel, whose managers are hidden away in offices behind the balcony. Their staff includes 26 cleaners, 24 usherettes, three box waiters, six security officers controlling the doors and carpark, and an interchanging 24-hour patrol of six firemen, who drop the solid iron safety curtain in the intervals and operate a tiny blue emergency light set unnoticeably seven feet up in the proscenium. Then there are the two bewigged and Georgian stage flunkeys, dressed in uniforms given second-hand by Buckingham Palace (theirs is an evening job – one is a mechanic, the other a drama student); and the two linkmen and twelve commissionaires, who for thirty-two years until his death in 1981 included ex-Sergeant-Major Martin of the Grenadier Guards, rooted like a redoubtable oak at the foot of the grand stairway.

The eight barmen are uniquely exposed to the audience – and the audience to them. The days of the week, they say, follow a variable graph from a faintly colourless Monday audience to the London sophisticates of mid-week (champagne, wine), grow dowdy again on Fridays, and on Saturdays pass into a generous clamour of night-outers (martini, soft drinks) driven in from the country. Mozart audiences are cultivated and polished; Wagnerians and Strauss-lovers often older, more intellectual; Verdians dress up.

The yearly consumption of 9,000 bottles of champagne, 100,000 whiskies, 100,000 gins and tonics, more than 30,000 bottles of wine and 6,000 lost or broken glasses suggests that the whole audience passes the evening in a state of sodden catalepsy. But in fact the figures work out sedately. The opera audiences are the wealthier, but the ballet rather abstemious and particular (they buy a lot of ice cream), and Saturday matinées, with their sprinkling of children, find affronted barmen solicited for Coca Cola.

Before the end of the decade, it is hoped, these multigrade audiences will be served in a second crush bar built out from the grand staircase mezzanine above cloakrooms and an orchestra rehearsal room. The future is full of such plans – an idea for improving the rake of the stalls; for clearing the view from the amphitheatre by lifting the false proscenium

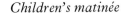

*Children's matinée*

and the fly-tower above it; for the reinstalment of a Victorian mechanism for adjusting the width of the proscenium. Into a yet mistier future the whole Royal Ballet and its Upper School may be brought together on this site.

The search is not only for finer, but for more performances. The Opera and Ballet – a unique double-treasury – jostle and cry for stage-space, but neither receives its due. And the fewer the performances, of course, the greater the tension when they come.

Yet it is precisely in release from such tension that the peculiar reward of dancer and singer lies. This freedom – the surrender to the music as its twin or instrument – occasionally touches a mysterious extreme. An unplanned self-oblivion, alighting in moments of technical mastery and musical beauty, is a phenomenon perfectly distinct among the finest performers. It comes, it seems, when the artist is unselfconsciously relaxed, and brings with it a sensation of lightness, even of emptiness, and of a perfect, choiceless accuracy. Two *Swan Lakes* and a *Manon* passed for Anthony Dowell like this, all of a piece. Kiri te Kanawa, in the last Act of *Arabella*, has three or four times thought herself the doll of some glorious ventriloquist ('I feel it's out of my hands, and that God has now given me just about everything.') Gundula Janowitz, during a few, rare arias and with characteristic precision, has felt levitated ten centimetres above the stage; and Lesley Collier, in the Rose Adagio of *The Sleeping Beauty*, was certain that the *corps* was physically holding her up. ('I didn't have to do a thing.')

The distressing aspect of such performances is that they pass unsensed by the audience. They are, it seems, a private exaltation, no better or worse than the artist's average. Excellence, stubbornly, still belongs to the conscious mind – but the mind which has the courage to trust to the music and to suppress the self. Occasionally, in both opera and ballet, such performances glow against a background of musical and technical splendour – orchestra, *corps de ballet*, house principals, chorus – and are united in a seemingly natural whole.

Britten's *Peter Grimes*, for instance, has become such a piece. Its spectrum of English character-studies, at once typical and individual, evokes an East Anglian fishing community in the last century, and involves the company so intimately that one or two members of the chorus have found themselves emotionally withdrawing from its depressive theme. Its gallery contains old Covent Garden favourites – Sir Geraint Evans, Heather Harper, John Dobson, the brassy landlady of Elizabeth Bainbridge, Forbes Robinson's heavy-handed magistrate, John Lanigan's faltering rector. Into this enclosed, amphibian community, with its false dignities and incestuous gossip, the outcast fisherman of Jon Vickers – a singer nurtured by Covent Garden since the 1950s – intrudes like a curse.

He enters the tavern of Act I with the blast of a storm behind him, and the community within – fishermen, town dignitaries, fishwives, prostitutes – freezes to a layer of uncomprehending faces: a moral void. In the embittered grandeur of his own savagery and solitude, tousled, massive, swathed in grey waterproof and sea-boots, he sings as if the people were not there at all – a mystical wondering at the heavens, floated on the unearthly note of E natural. The drinking townsmen, steeped in their heartiness, their sexual by-play and hypocrisy, stare at him in silence. He sings of the Great Bear and the Pleiades. '*Who, who can turn skies back and begin again?*'

The notes fall softly, eerily, as if from a great height, like moonlight breaking over water. In the pit, Colin Davis elicits a simmering whisper of sound, mouthing the words. (He loves this moment: 'You turn a corner, and things aren't quite the same as they were.') In the auditorium the difference between the silence of an empty theatre and the hush of a full one is suddenly immense.

But the next second Vickers's voice fills with rancour. He becomes bullish again, a shambling, haunted ruin of a man, fists clenched and shaking, huger and worse than those around him, singing the refrain of the outsider, unheard. But then this outburst leaves him stilled. He cannot touch the others. They think him either drunk or mad. So his voice rises in quiet again, disembodied, awed, sucked away, while the orchestra slithers to a bottom C and the hatted and bonnetted faces around him remain those in which a man looks despairingly for any breath of human light.

Such a performance seems inseparable from its portrayer; yet the role was composed for Peter Pears, a far different tenor, who declaimed the song on this stage with a fragile poetry of his own. Those for whom an opera or a ballet has been created possess it in a special way. In particular, the body and temperament of its first performer are a dance's fountainhead, and the Ballet has poured on to the stage a procession of first casts which may echo round a work long after they have gone. MacMillan's *The Rite of Spring*, premiered in 1962, would long ago have passed to the next generation had it not been created for Monica Mason when she was only twenty.

To the awesome ceremony of Stravinsky's music, a tribal ritual of earth-worship, danced by a *corps* of forty and set by Sidney Nolan in primordial desert, culminates in the choosing and death of a sacrificial virgin. Dressed in blotched body-stockings of crimson and orange, their faces whitened and hieratically daubed, the men's heads sprout Japanese topknots and the women's drip with straw manes black-tipped like those of horses.

While the opening movement mounts in an implacable whirlwind of strings and staccato trumpets, Mason is running lightly in the half-darkness of the wings, her costume covered by an old green cardigan and leggings. Then the music stops abruptly. The lights go out. Through the audience there rustles a faint, uneasy murmuring, as if it were a wind waiting to be stilled by the lonely power of this dancer now walking out of the wings.

The lights go up on a tribal semicircle under a blue sky. Above the cinnamon-coloured wilderness of a prehistoric time, Nolan's central symbol – phallus or gold-white moon – lifts in a huge, pre-nuclear mushroom-cloud over the reddish wastes. Soon Mason, marked for death, lies like a wounded animal downstage. Her eyes, immolated in ash-white make-up, show lustrous and immense. She rises, bows, caresses her straw mane of hair in farewell – farewell to her beauty – and is passed like a totem or a mummy above the line of the men, as if she were already dead. Finally, lifted up to the simmering music in postures of alternate pathos and command, she becomes at once victim and goddess and tribe incarnate.

Then the death-music begins. It is like a terrible, unstoppable rhythm of the blood. The tribe gyrates around her in orgasmic cavortings and simian leg-liftings and daemonic twirls, while she runs frenzied among them. As they lie spreadeagled over the stage, their legs and arms split and close in a feverish sea. The orchestra is hushed to a throb of woodwind and tambourine, while she, arms raised, palms bent outwards, skips between them with a phantasmal lightness and terror – a child or a spirit dancing to the air.

But the quiet does not last. Slowly Nolan's moon reddens to scarlet, like the blush on some blank yet all-seeing face, and she starts her dance to die. The movements are still natural to her which were choreographed on her body almost two decades before – 'I felt I was back in my childhood, in Africa, just dancing' – and she fills them with a lonely and impassioned grandeur unique to herself. She has the cherished gift of absolute musicality. She is the music in motion. It drives her like a tempest. She circles the stage in panic-stricken leaps and spins, arms flailing, jerks and buckles as if the breath were leaving her. Her face becomes a mask of terror and exhaustion and a speechless prayer for life. Her hair sweeps the ground. The orchestra torments the stage with pecking decrescendoes and drum-throbs. As she weakens, the tribe crawls voraciously towards her. Their legs and hands quiver with impatience. Her arms fly out in useless supplication. She seems to try to thrust them away, then falls writhing, rises again. But now her gestures have become loose and wild. Dying, she is being sucked back into the tribal life-stream, into nature itself, falls again with a thud of drums, and is tossed like a leaf into the sky.

In the very midst of the applause, the mind of the singer or dancer may be engaged in a ruthless post-mortem. As the curtain falls it perhaps brings with it a breath of vindication, but no sense of safety or of permanence. Meanwhile, after the illusion of gazing on another world, the audience departs with the half-conscious sensation that this world continues after they have gone, that it has somehow been established. But of course it has not, it was created only for them, and after their departure the artists pick up their flowers and pad away to the squalor of their dressing-rooms. The beauty which they inhabited, but could not see, belongs now to the audience.

*Sergeant Martin*

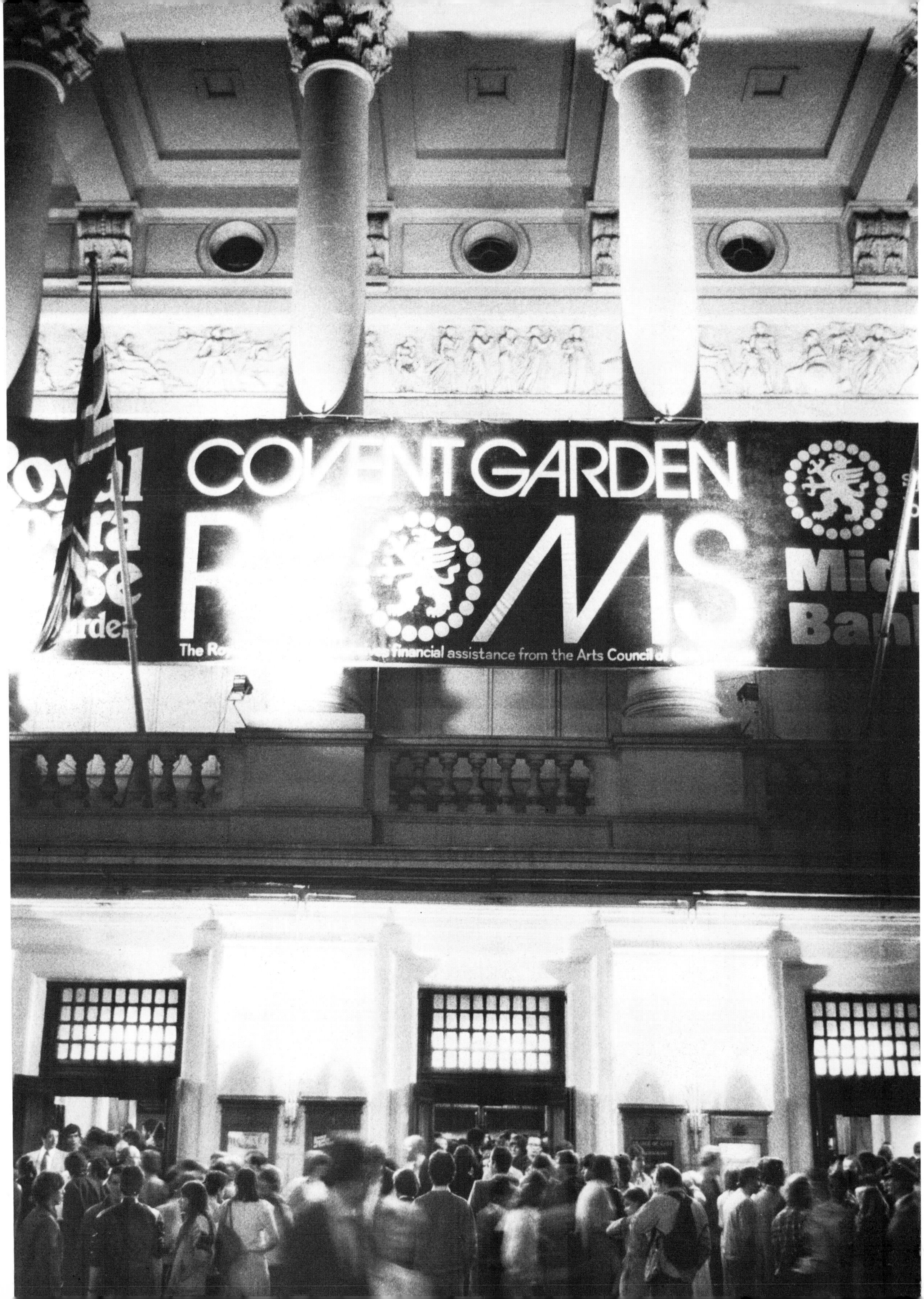
COVENT GARDEN
financial assistance from the Arts

**Così fan tutte**. Ruggero Raimondi arrives in the women's dressing-rooms to hug and tease Agnes Baltsa, seated with her husband before she goes on stage as Dorabella, opposite, with Kiri te Kanawa as Fiordiligi

Recovering offstage. Sir Colin Davis with his wife Shamsi
in his Opera House suite during an interval; and Lucia
Popp in the wings, before returning on stage as Susanna in
*Le nozze di Figaro*

Colin Davis conducting *Così fan tutte*

During performance: usherettes and nurses

Left: Kiri te Kanawa and Agnes Baltsa, sitting, with Daniela Mazzucato as Despina in *Così fan tutte*; Kiri te Kanawa returning to her dressing-room; the stage crew supervisor and a technical manager checking the set's alignment before curtain-up on *Le nozze di Figaro*.

Overleaf: *Le nozze di Figaro*. As principals take curtain calls after Act II, stage staff and prop men are already changing the scenery, and a charge hand signalling to the fly gallery to lower the curving draperies

Opposite: Robert Lloyd, his head monstrously enlarged by the wigmaster's pate, dressing for Fiesco in *Simon Boccanegra*

The audience

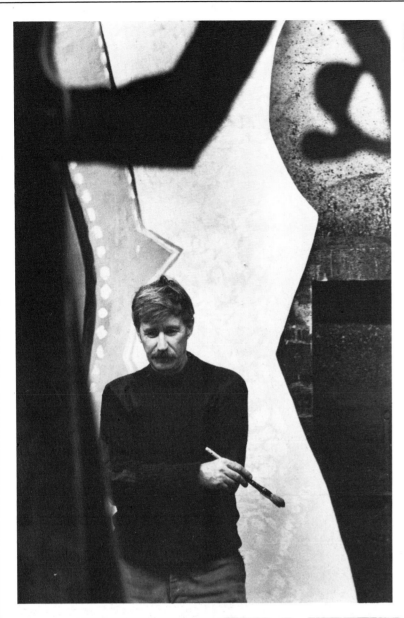

**Daphnis and Chloë.**
Opposite: John Craxton, the original designer of *Daphnis and Chloë* in 1951, returns to repaint his scenery thirty years later.
Opposite below: two prop men hanging the tinselled net which sparkles behind the background 'sea'

Below: Michael Somes, who danced Daphnis in 1951, coaching Marguerite Porter; the administrative, ballet and technical staff consulting on stage after rehearsal

**Daphnis and Chloë.** Shepherdesses quarrel with the scenery in rehearsal; Anthony Dowell as Daphnis

**Isadora.** Opposite: Sandra Conley in performance, photographed through the gauze from the back of the stage

**The Firebird**. Derek Rencher in his dressing-room,
preparing to become the Immortal Kostcheï

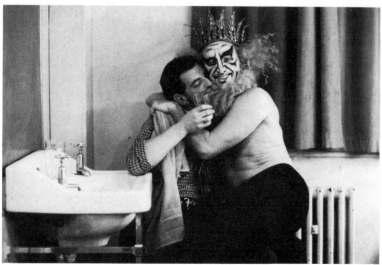

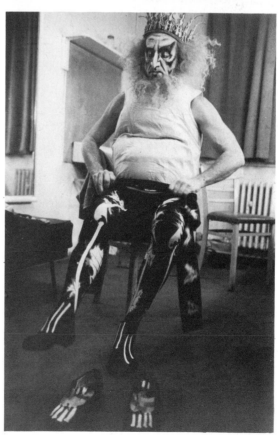

**The Firebird**. Derek Rencher as Kostcheï, in rehearsal, top, and performance, his cloak flared out by a dresser as he stalks on from the wings

**Giselle** in rehearsal. Opposite: Norman Morrice, with Jill Gregory and Christopher Newton, coaching Marguerite Porter; Anthony Dowell, with Graham Fletcher; ballet and wardrobe staff on stage, in discussion after dress rehearsal

**Giselle**. Anthony Dowell, in a prop room in the wings, rehearsing the taking of his wreath to Giselle's grave; at curtain call with Makarova; fans crowd the stage door for Makarova's autograph

**Tristan und Isolde**. Opposite: Colin Davis revises a passage with Berit Lindholm in her dressing-room during an interval. Overleaf: lighting the set

**Lohengrin**. Overleaf: matters of timing. An assistant stage manager prepares to cue on Heather Harper (Elsa) and her attendants; the assistant chorus master conducts from a concealed perch behind stage flats

**Parsifal**. Georg Solti conducts; with Peter Hofmann in rehearsal, and Yvonne Minton as Kundry

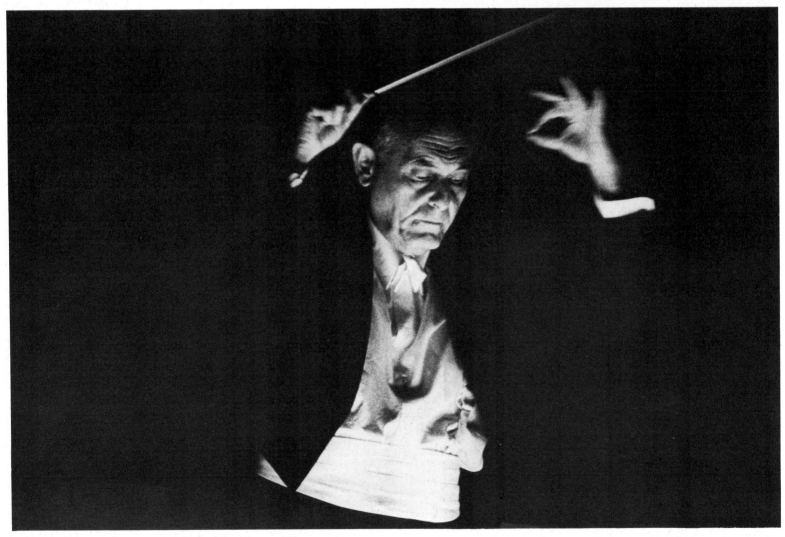

The Royal Ballet fiftieth anniversary celebrations. Top: Sadler's Wells Royal Ballet director Peter Wright, seated beside Kenneth MacMillan at rehearsals for the gala. Bottom: members of Sadler's Wells Royal Ballet in *Coppélia* with Margaret Barbieri and David Bintley; and in the Opera House canteen

Opposite above: the *corps de ballet* in *La Bayadère*. Below: after *The Sleeping Beauty*, Ninette de Valois with Frederick Ashton, Kenneth MacMillan and Norman Morrice, in a rain of daffodils

The Royal Ballet fiftieth anniversary. Below: Dame Margot
Fonteyn at the annual cutting of the Taglioni cake; and
members of Sadler's Wells Royal Ballet before curtain-up
on *The Two Pigeons*. Right: Sadler's Wells Royal Ballet in
*Les Patineurs*; Margot Fonteyn visiting the dressing-rooms;
celebrations in the Crush Bar afterwards

Opposite: Jessye Norman about to take the stage for a Sunday recital

**Un ballo in maschera**. Montserrat Caballé and Luciano Pavarotti backstage; and right, Caballé (Amelia) encouraged by Pavarotti (Gustavus III) from the wings

236

**Lucrezia Borgia**. John Copley, principal resident producer, jokes with Joan Sutherland over a point of characterisation in the banquet scene, with Alfredo Kraus looking on; banners and flowers at the première

240

**Cinderella**. Derek Rencher and Brian Shaw as the Ugly
Sisters, Wayne Sleep as the Jester. Below: wardrobe staff
give running repairs to Derek Rencher's Ugly Sister; the
audience waits; the ballet stage managers carry dancers'
flowers to the dressing-rooms

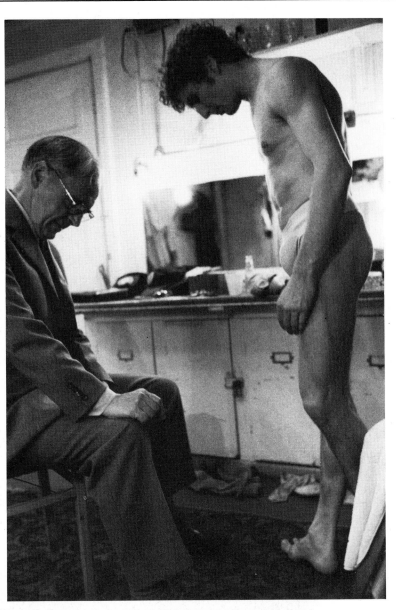

Opposite: a dancer in the wings softens her slipper's
papier-mâché head; the international orthopaedic surgeon
Eivind Thomasen examines Wayne Eagling in his
dressing-room; a dancer practises behind the backcloth

**Mayerling**. Lesley Collier as Mary Vetsera, David Wall as
Prince Rudolf

Bryony Brind, right, checking her costume for *Scènes de Ballet*; Lesley Collier, below, with assistant ballet mistress Rosalind Eyre; the *corps* in *Les Sylphides*

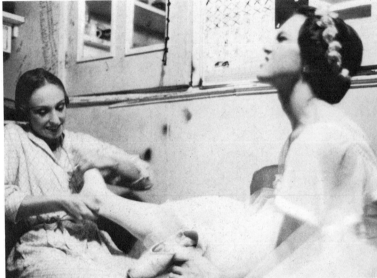

**Peter Grimes** in rehearsal. Jon Vickers (Grimes) takes over the coaching of the boy actor who will play his apprentice. The child must leave Grimes' cliffside hut to die in a fall, but in reality he descends a ladder out of sight of the audience, to the scream of a boy soprano.

Opposite above: view from the rear of the stage; below: Patricia Payne (Mrs. Sedley) chatting before her stage entrance. Overleaf: *Peter Grimes* in performance. The deputy stage manager leafs through a score by the prompt corner control panel during Act II, after members of the chorus are cued on intermittently, and John Dobson (Bob Boles), in an ever-mounting tension, rants against Grimes. Act III: a fisherman rests in the wings among *Don Giovanni* statuary

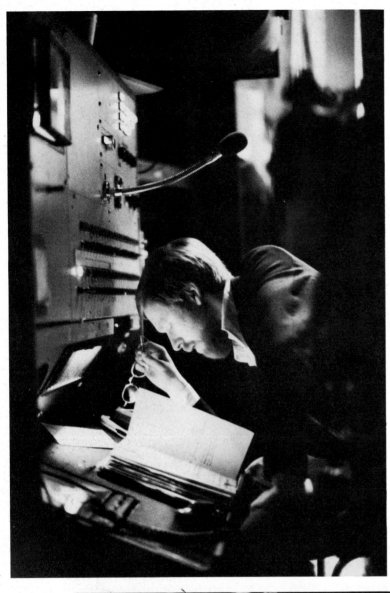

**The Rite of Spring** in rehearsal and performance, with
Monica Mason as the Chosen Maiden

**The Rite of Spring**. Monica Mason in performance, and relaxing in her dressing-room with Kenneth and Deborah MacMillan

# INDEX

*Africaine, L'*: 146, 158
*Aida*: 68
*Alceste*: 63, 64
Allan, Richard Van: *93, 200*
Allen, Thomas: 65, *196*
*Anastasia*: 63, 65
Anderson, Ande: *152, 185*
Andrew, HRH Prince: 99
*Arabella*: 203
Armstrong, Karan: *36, 38–40, 42*
Armstrong, Sir Robert: 21
Arts Council: 21, 24
Ashton, Sir Frederick: 24, 25, 55, 57, 58, 59, 68, 100, 107, 148, 159, 160, 162, *164–5, 167, 169, 171–2, 183*, 195, 233

Bainbridge, Elizabeth: 203
Baker, Dame Janet: 64, 145, 191
Balanchine, George: 107
*Ballo in maschera, Un*: 146, *236*
Baltsa, Agnes: *208–9, 213*
Barbieri, Margaret: *232*
Barry, Edward: 12
Baryshnikov, Mikhail: *162, 165–6, 170, 172*
Batchelor, Michael: *94*
*Bayadère, La*: *233*
Bayreuth: 146
BBC: 21, 24
Beagley, Stephen: *122*
Bedford, Dukes of: 12, 14
Beecham, Sir Thomas: 12, 14, 18, 108
Bennett, Richard Rodney: 76, 102
Bergsma, Deanne: 25
Berio, Luciano: 24
*Biches, Les*: *161*
*Billy Budd*: 18
Bintley, David: *232*
Björnson, Maria: 64, *81–2*
*Bohème, La*: 17, 68, *147*, 154
Böhm, Karl: 108
Bolshoi: 13, 21, 201
*Boris Godunov*: 159
Bournonville, August: 107
Brind, Bryony: 25, *244*
Bruson, Renato: *114, 117, 119*
Bryan, Robert: *37*
Bumbry, Grace: 17, 159
Burrows, Stuart: 17, 73, 103

Caballé, Montserrat: *236*
Callas, Maria: 12, 159
Carreras, José: *34*
Caruso, Enrico: 12, 17, 19
Chadwick, Fiona: 25, *44*
Chaliapin, Feodor: 12
Chitty, Stella: *38*, 103, *116*, 151, 154
*Cinderella*: 159, *240–1*
Coleman, Michael: *52*, *94*
Coliseum, London: 146
Collier, Lesley: 26, *53, 94, 98*, 99, 163, *165, 169–70*, 191, 195, 203, *243, 244*
Comelli, Attilio: 21
Conley, Sandra: 101, *221*
Connor, Laura: *79*
*Contes d'Hoffmann, Les*: 62, 64, 65, 68, *69–70, 80–91*, 107, 112

Copley, John: 63, 104, *238*
*Coppélia*: 112, *232*
*Cosi fan tutte*: 73, *208–9, 211, 213*
Cotrubus, Ileana: 65, *91*
Cowie, Edward: 24
Craxton, John: *218*
Crush Bar: 13, 18, *19, 20*, 80, *136, 235*

Dali, Salvador: 21
*Dances of Albion*: 162
*Daphnis and Chloë*: 146, 192, *218–20*
Davis, Sir Colin: 21, 24, 25, *36, 54, 92*, 103, *111, 131, 139*, 154, *198–9*, 200, 203, 210, 211, 227
Deane, Derek: *46*
Dobson, John: *175*, 203, *248*
Domingo, Placido: 17, *81*, 87, 90, *184–7*
*Don Carlos*: 146, 159
*Don Giovanni*: 63, *103–4, 109*, 112, *126–35, 144–5*, 158, 200
*Donnerstag*: 24
Doran, Adrian: *23*
Dowell, Anthony: 26, 48, 50, 57, 99, *182–3*, 203, 220, *225–6*
Downes, Edward: *106*
*Dream, The*: 68
Dudley, William: 62, 64, *128–9*

Eagling, Wayne: 26, 28, 44, 53, 98, 99, *125*, 160, 192, *242*
Edwards, Leslie: *47*, 55
*Elektra*: 110, 201
Ellis, Wendy: *45, 96, 99*
*Enigma Variations*: 154
*Eugene Onegin*: 18
Evans, Sir Geraint: *81*, 87, 203
Everding, August: 159
Eyre, Rosalind: *244*
*Falstaff*: 55, 201
*Fanciulla del West, La*: 55, *56*, 66
Farmer, Peter: 63
*Faust*: 12
Fenice, La: 13
*Fidelio*: 108
*Fille Mal Gardée, La*: 159, 192
Findlay, Paul: 21, *139*
*Firebird, The*: 162, 194, *222–4*
*Fledermaus, Die*: 21, 68
Fletcher, Graham: *75, 183, 225*
Floral Hall: *158–9*
Fonteyn, Dame Margot: 12, 25, 162, *235*
Frank, Jonathan: *32*
*Freischütz, Der*: 55, 157
Freni, Mirella: *147*
Friedrich, Götz: *35–6, 38–9*, 62, 157, *175*
Friends of Covent Garden: 19

Gardelli, Lamberto: *153*
Gardini, Ubaldo: 103, *132–3*
George IV, King: 12
George VI, King: 12
Georgiadis, Nicholas: 62, 63
Ghiuselev, Nicola: *80*
*Giselle*: 18, 50, 150, *225–6*
Giulini, Carlo Maria: 55, 108

*Gloria*: 66, 100, *121–5*
Gobbi, Tito: 12
Goodall, Reginald: 71, *72*
Gray, Keith: 76, 101, 102, 142, 151, *241*
Gregory, Jill: 24, 49, 160, 193, 225
Gregson, Richard: *83*
Grisi, Giulia: 19
*Götterdämmerung*: 157

Haitink, Bernard: 108
*Hamlet*: *182–3*
Harper, Heather: 203, *229*
Helpmann, Robert: *182–3*
*Hermanas, Las*: 58
Hofmann, Peter: *176, 230*
Hosking, Julian: *75, 122*, 150
Howe, Judith: *74*
Howell, Gwynne: 54, 72, 80, *103–4*, 145

*Ice Break, The*: 154
Inkin, Sally: *75*
*Invitation, The*: 58
*Isadora*: *51*, 59, 61, *74–9*, 100–2, 142, 149, 194

Janowitz, Gundula: 103, 203
Jefferies, Stephen: 26, *75*, 101, 192

Kabaivanska, Raina: *93*
Kanawa, Kiri te: 17, 103–4, *133–4, 139*, 203, 208, 213
Karczykowski, Ryszard: *39*
Kay, Barry: 63, 76, 102, 142
*King Priam*: 24
King's Smoking Room: 13
Kirkland, Gelsey: *94, 97–8*
Kirov: 201
Kleiber, Carlos: 108, *185*
Klemperer, Otto: 108
Kraus, Alfredo: *238*

Lanigan, John: 203
Larsen, Gerd: 18, 24, *32*, 53, *94–5*, 160, 193
Law, Iris: *167*
Lawrence, Ashley: *19*, 102
Leggate, Robin: *38*, 42
Ligeti, Gyorgy: 24
Lindholm, Berit: *180–1*, 227
Linos, Glenys: 36
Lloyd, Robert: *114*, 217
*Lohengrin*: 24, 62, 65, 112, 146, 150, 154, *229*
*Lucrezia Borgia*: 18, *238*
*Luisa Miller*: 14, 154
*Lulu*: *35–42*, 62, 63, 154

Maazel, Lorin: 108
Macarthur, Tom: 61, *174*
*Macbeth*: *104–5*, 107, *113–120*, 146–7, 154, 197
McCarthy, John: 104, 108
McGee, Bill: *38*
McIntyre, Donald: 64, *176, 180–1*, 191
MacMillan, Kenneth: 25, 55, 57–9, *58*, 61, 62, 74–6, 78, 99, 100–2, *121*, 142, 148, 190, 195, 204, *232*, 233, *253*

*Madama Butterfly*: 17, *93*, 158
Mahler, Gustave: 12
Makarova, Natalia: *50, 226*
Manen, Hans van: 55, 58
*Manon*: 33, 57, 61, *62–3*, 154, 203
Margaret, HRH Princess: *22, 172*
*Marguerite and Armand*: 194
Mario, Giovanni: 19
Markova, Dame Alicia: 22
Martin, Sergeant: 201, *205, 207*
Mason, Monica: 25, 26, 28, 58, 59, 79, 100, 101, *182*, 191, *204–5, 250, 252–3*
*Mayerling*: 52, 57, 58, 61, 63, 65, 148, *243*
Mazzucato, Daniela: *213*
Mehta, Zubin: 108, *110*
Melba, Dame Nellie: 12, 17
Messiaen, Oliver: 24
Metropolitan Opera: 17, 21, 146, 201
Milcheva, Alexandrina: *152–3*
Miller, Mary: *74*
Minton, Yvonne: *231*
Molyneux, Anthony: *123*
Moran, Linda: *123*
Morrell, Peter: *186*
Morrice, Norman: 25, *54–5*, 102, 149, *169*, 193, 225, 233
Moser, Sir Claus: 21, *22–3*
Moser, Eda: 65
*Moses and Aaron*: 159
Moshinsky, Elijah: *104–5*, 107, *114, 116, 120*, 146–7
Musgrave, Thea: 24
Muti, Riccardo: 105, 107, 108, *114–6, 118*, 146–7
*My Brother, My Sisters*: 58, 149

*Ned Kelly*: 24
Newton, Christopher: *33, 165, 167, 193, 225*
*Noces, Les*: 162, 191
Nolan, Sir Sidney: 24, 204
*Norma*: 151, *152–3*
Norman, Jessye: *237*
*Nozze di Figaro, Le*: 104, *196, 210, 213–5*
Nureyev, Rudolf: 25

O'Brien, Timothy: *36–7*, 62
Oman, Julia Trevelyan: 61
Opéra, Paris: 17, 21, 24, 146
*Otello*: 17, 68, 157, *184–7*

Paisey, Karen: *28*
Park, Merle: 25, 26, *58, 59, 61, 74–5, 78, 94, 97–8*, 100, 101, 149, 194
Parker, Monica: 59
*Parsifal*: 157, *197, 230–1*
*Patineurs, Les*: *235*
Patti, Adelina: 12, 19
Pavarotti, Luciano: *236*
Payne, Patricia: *247*
Pears, Peter: 204
Penney, Jennifer: 26, *45, 122, 190*
*Peter Grimes*: 24, 62, 107, 158, *203–4, 246–9*
Petipa, Marius: 107

Phillips, Jeffrey: *37, 129*, 142
*Playground*: 57
Pradier, Winnie: 201
Prêtre, Georges: *83–4*
Popp, Lucia: *210*
Porter, Marguerite: 26, *30–1, 45, 161, 182, 219, 225*
Povey, Jean: *117, 186*

Queen Mother, the: *169, 172*

Raimondi, Ruggero: 103–4, *133–4*, 145, *200, 209*
*Rake's Progress, The*: 18, 112
Rambert, Dame Marie: *172*
Read, John B: 142, 150
Reich, Günter: *38, 40*
Remedios, Alberto: *175*
Rencher, Derek: 48, *53, 74, 97, 222–4, 240–1*
Rennison, Michael: 36
Reszke, Jean & Edouard de: 12
*Rhapsody*: 162, *164–73*
*Rheingold, Das*: *174, 178*
Ricciarelli, Katia: *191*
Rich, John: 12
Richter, Hans: 12
*Ring des Nibelungen, Der*: 12, 64, 71, *110–1*, 154, 157, *174–81*
*Rite of Spring, The*: 100, 162, *163, 191, 204–5, 250–3*

Robinson, Forbes: 203
*Romeo and Juliet*: 63, 66, 71, *94–9*
*Rosenkavalier, Der*: 159

Sadler's Wells Royal Ballet: 21, *55, 232, 235*
Saedén, Erik: *42*
Sallinen, Aulis: 24
Salminen, Matti: *177*
*Salome*: 21, *55, 68*
Sandilands, Sir Francis: *136*
Sanjust, Filippo: 61
Savonlinna Festival: 24
Scala, La: 13, 21, 146
*Scènes de Ballet*: 244
Schlesinger, John: 62, 64, *80, 83*
Schmidt, Helga: *102, 131, 152*
Scholar, Betty: *131*
Scotto, Renata: 105, *114*, 197
Serra, Luciana: *86*
*Seven Deadly Sins, The*: 63
Seymour, Lynn: 25, 59
Shaw, Brian: *240*
Sibley, Antoinette: 25, *57, 195*
*Siegfried*: *154, 157, 178*
*Simon Boccanegra*: 68, *217*
Sleep, Wayne: *240*
*Sleeping Beauty, The*: 19, *44–7, 49, 55,* 148, 154, *195, 203, 221, 233*

*Solitaire*: 63
Solti, Sir Georg: 21, *108, 230*
Somes, Michael: 24, *49, 97, 160, 162, 193, 219*
*Sonnambula, La*: 19
Spurling, Ian: 63
Staatsoper, Vienna: 21, 55, 111
Stade, Frederica von: *193*
Stennett, Michael: 63
Stockhausen, Karlheinz: 24
Sutherland, Dame Joan: *238–9*
Svoboda, Josef: 157
*Swan Lake*: 14, *48–50, 53, 65,* 71, 110, *163, 191, 203*
*Sylphides, Les*: *160, 244*
*Symphonic Variations*: 160, 162

Tear, Robert: 86
Tetley, Glen: 55, 59
*Thérèse*: 112
Thomasen, Eivind: *242*
Tippett, Sir Michael: 21
Tomlinson, John: *133*
Tooley, Sir John: 21, *22–3*, 24, 54, 61, *102, 116, 139,* 148, 149, *153, 169, 185, 200*
*Tosca*: 71, 146, *155,* 159, *188–9*
*Traviata, La*: 12
*Tristan und Isolde*: 18, *110*
Trust, Royal Opera House: 24
Tudor, Antony: 58

*Two Pigeons, The*: 235

Valois, Dame Ninette de: 22, 24, *43, 44, 55, 58, 101, 233*
Verrett, Shirley: *188*
Vickers, Jon: *110*, 203–4, 246
Victoria, Queen: 14, *14*
Visconti, Luchino: 21
*Voluntaries*: 162

Walker, David: 63
Walker, Nina: *72, 73*
*Walküre, Die*: 157, *179–81*
Wall, David: 26, *30–1, 33, 52, 78, 191, 243*
Walter, Bruno: 12
Webster, Sir David: 14, 19, 21
Wells, Doreen: *191*
*Werther*: 18, *34*
Whitten, Rosalyn: *49*
Wood, Peter: 103–4, *131, 145*
Wordsworth, Barry: *76,* 102
*Wozzeck*: 158
Wright, Peter: *232*
Wylde, Pippa: 25, *51*

Young, Emanuel: 96

*Zauberflöte, Die*: 71, 159
Zeffirelli, Franco: 21, 159

# Acknowledgements

Besides those acknowledged in the introduction, the photographer and author are especially grateful to the following: Jennifer Adey, Ande Anderson, John Bacon, Dame Janet Baker, Kim Baker, Frank Barker, John Barker, Stella Beddard, Michael Becket, Sir Isaiah Berlin, Maria Björnson, Mark Bonham Carter, Stanley Booth, Lynn Bradbury, John Bradley, Jonah Bray, Wally Bridges, Bryony Brind, Michael Brown, Peter Brownlee, Stuart Burrows, Albert Cain, John Charlton, Nick Chelton, Max Clarke, Larry Coke, Lesley Collier, Sandra Conley, Valerie Connell, Stanley Cooper, Peter Courtier, John Cruickshank, Robin Dartington, Nat Diamond, John Dobson, Graham Dove, Duncan Dow, Anthony Dowell, Edward Downes, David Drew, Linda Duxbury, John Edwards, Leslie Edwards, Sir Geraint Evans, Terry Fitton, Susan Foll, Francesca Franchi, Fred Frankham, Lamberto Gardelli, Ubaldo Gardini, Bram Gay, Reginald Goodall, Leonard C. Grant, Jill Gregory, Richard Gregson, Bill Griffin, Bill Hall, Aydin Hasirci, Nicholas Heyward, Nicholas Hooton, Gwynne Howell, Christine Hurst, Terry Jackson, Waheb Jaulen, Stephen Jefferies, Corrine Jones, Janet Judd, Kiri te Kanawa, Barry Kay, Terry Keen, Malcolm Kinch, Jane Lambert, Gerd Larsen, Ashley Lawrence, Ted Lipscombe, Tony Mabbutt, Terry Mardon, Janet Mayo, John McCarthy, Alex McDonald, Donald McIntyre, Robert McPherson, Stephen Mead, James Monahan, Bob Moore, Stephen Moore, Norman Morrice, Sir Claus Moser, John Moyle, Charles Murland, Jack Musto, Christopher Newton, Charlie Niclas, Timothy O'Brien, Merle Park, Jennifer Penney, Edward Percival, Jean Percival, Winnie Pradier, Eric Pressley, Janice Pullen, John B. Read, Derek Rencher, Christopher Renshaw, Henry Roche, Betty Scholar, Stephen Scragg, Jennie Selby, Lynn Seymour, Antoinette Sibley, Maurits Sillem, Charles Spencer, Nicki Spencer, Clifford Starr, Terry Stacey, Michael Stennett, Jeremy Sutcliffe, Oliver Symons, David Syrus, R. Temple Savage, Glen Tetley, Honor Thackrah, John Thomas, Alan Thorne, Noel Tobin, Julio Trebilcock, Anthony Twiner, Kathy Valentine, David Walker, Nina Walker, Tom Walker, David Wall, Tom Wall, Michael Whiteley, Brian Withnell, Peter Wood, Christine Woodward, Barry Wordsworth, Faith Worth, Peter Wright.
And for generous professional encouragement and advice: Penny Hoare of Hamish Hamilton, Graham Wainwright of Leeds Cameras, and Spencer Colour Lab.